ANTIQUES

A Popular Guide to Antiques for Everyone

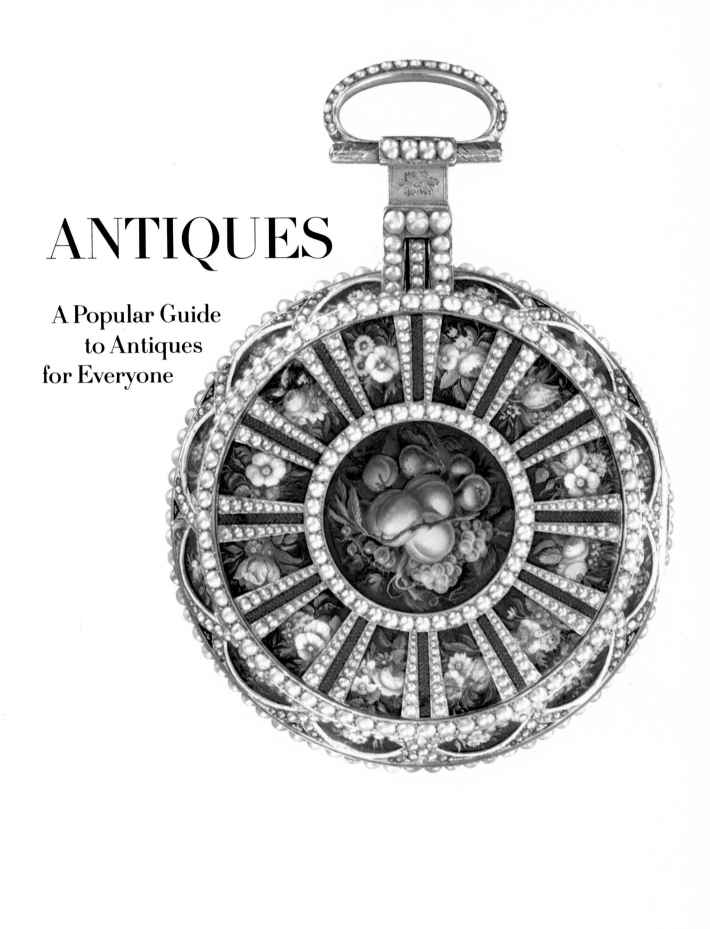

ANTIQUES

A Popular Guide
to Antiques
for Everyone

Introduction
by
Peter Philp

Galley Press

This edition published 1980 by
Cathay Books Limited
59 Grosvenor Street, London W1.

© 1980 Cathay Books
Reprinted 1982
ISBN 0 904644 47 2

Produced by Mandarin Publishers Limited,
22a, Westlands Road,
Quarry Bay, Hong Kong

Printed in Singapore

CONTENTS

1

INTRODUCTION

2

There are two basic reasons for buying antiques: one, because you like them, the other because you may hope to make money out of them. Many other motives, more subtle and high-minded can be put forward, such as helping to preserve the heritage of the past, or creating a harmonious background for living. Yet in the end, it is the pleasure of personal possession, coupled perhaps, with the prospect of profit, that sets most of us searching – for what?

We do not always know until we find it, and even then we sometimes feel unsure, wishing we had more knowledge, doubting our ability to discriminate, infallibly or by flair alone, between good and bad, genuine and fake.

This book sets out to provide some of the basic facts, without which bargain-hunting can be an expensive, even if amusing, pastime. The inexperienced buyer is certainly far safer in the hands of a reputable dealer, willing to guarantee the authenticity of what he is selling, than foraging in street-market and junk-store.

As for the auction-room, the atmosphere is a heady one, requiring great self-discipline if a sensible limit is not to be exceeded in face of stiff competition. Except when backed by the expertise of the big auctioneers, catalogue descriptions sometimes deserve to be on the shelves of a lending library, reserved for romantic fiction. Most dangerous of all is the *private buy*, resulting from a classified advertisement, which is likely to prove at best a sad case of the blind leading the blind, and at worst a near-criminal confidence trick.

The ever-increasing interest in antiques and bric-à-brac over the last few years has led to a mushroom growth of shops large and small. There are also covered markets where many of the tiny booths are tenanted by part-timers, huddled together to attract the maximum passing trade and, in some places, such as in New York, to provide mutual protection against those who collect antiques at gun point; and fairs where dealers gather to exhibit their wares for a limited period – anything from two days to a fortnight.

The standards among all these are, as might be expected, variable. At the best fairs the individual exhibitors take pride in presenting the cream of their stock, and before it is put on sale it is ruthlessly vetted by committees of experts, so that both buyer and seller are reasonably safe, even from genuine mistakes in description. At the worst fairs the general level of quality can be lamentably low, but the well-trained

eye can still sometimes spot a worthwhile buy.

Much the same is true of the open markets, reminiscent of eastern bazaars, that now stretch from Paris, where there are five, to Bermondsey and Portobello in London, and from Helsingborg in Sweden (open for about ten days only in the early part of August) to scattered centres on the West Coast of America. Much of the merchandise offered for sale in these flea-markets is rubbish, but it is still possible to find genuine pieces at very realistic prices, if you have knowledge and do not mind staying up late at night or getting up early in the morning (a good time to be at Bermondsey is three a.m.). Though some of the traders are undoubted rogues, and others are out-of-work actresses making up in charm what they lack in erudition, there is a hard core of market-traders who are honest, industrious and well-informed, many of them young people, serving their apprenticeship in a tough school, who frequently go on to graduate as established and highly respected dealers. And some of them remember, with gratitude, old customers who bought from them when all they had in the world was a barrow in the street, and a few bits of battered metalwork or chipped china.

The systematic acquisition of antiques is, like most other human activities, largely a matter of learning to get along with the other people whose business or hobby it is. It can be highly entertaining, very exciting, sometimes frustrating, occasionally calamitous. Much disappointment can be avoided if the buyer tries to learn all he can about the subject that particularly interests him, and clears his mind, early on, of popular misconceptions. Age alone does not necessarily make a thing valuable. It usually needs, also, to be good of its kind. In the eye of the budding collector, beauty is often confused with superficial prettiness, and it may take time and effort to appreciate purity of line and form.

Rarity does not always go hand in hand with excellence, but the *advanced* collector often prizes uniqueness above all else – and does so with a passion that appears all but paranoiac to family, friends, and even to other collectors who are equally hell-bent, but on a different route. Never expect too much sympathy from other addicts. The specialist, liable to be labelled a fanatic by the aesthete, is ready to castigate as a mere *decorator* the collector who wants his home to be a home rather than a museum, and chooses antiques for their usefulness and pleasing qualities.

On the financial side, investment is easily muddled with speculation. A collector invests, a dealer speculates. These roles frequently overlap, become reversed or interchanged, but the principle remains the same. The price of certain classes of antiques having risen rapidly of recent years, it has been possible with little effort and less learning to make handsome profits over a short term; but there is a distinct danger that antiques, if treated too much like stocks and shares, will also behave like them.

Allowing for inevitable rises and falls due to shifts of fashion, most antiques show a steady appreciation over the years and, in the USA at least, can in some cases be bequeathed to museums so as to make a major saving in taxation at the end of the collector's own lifetime. But while he lives, the real dividend on his investment ought surely to be seen as the immense satisfaction to be gained by seeking out, and treasuring for a while, the splendid array of things that other men have made and left for him to enjoy.

1 *Louis XVI tulipwood games table, mounted in Sèvres porcelain, stamped* M Carlin, JME. *This exceptionally fine piece of French furniture was sold by the Marquess of Lansdowne at Sotheby's, London, in 1970 for £54,000 ($140,400).*

2 *Hard-paste porcelain vase, painted in enamel colours with the Flowers of the Seasons, the plum tree, peony, lotus and chrysanthemum in the palette of the* famille verte *on a black ground,* famille noire. *Chinese, reign of the Emperor K'ang Hsi.*

3 *Louis XV commode, made by J Schmitz. Veneered in tulipwood and Kingwood and mounted in ormolu, this fine example of French furniture was in the collection of the late Mrs Anna Thomson Dodge of Rose Terrace, Grosse Pointe Farms, Michigan, USA and was sold at Christie's, London, in 1971 for 7,500 guineas ($20,475).*

This is an attempt to clear some of the confusion from the minds of those who think they like antique furniture, but do not know their Gothic from their Rococo.

Although styles of furniture from the earliest times were very individual according to locality, there were designs that were international, spreading from town to town, country to country, continent to continent – sometimes quickly, sometimes slowly. About twenty-five years time-lag is usually allowed when dating a provincial piece of international design but this can prove a very unreliable guide. Whereas some of the furniture made in the country towns of Britain and France in the early 19th century shows only the most naïve attempt, if any, to keep abreast of the times, much of that made in New York would have been accepted as being in the height of fashion in London or Paris, all of it consciously based on designs taken from the ancient world of Egypt, Greece and Rome. **4**

And for good reason. These styles recur throughout history and have formed the basis for many different fashions. From about 1500 BC onwards, the Egyptians had beds, stools, chairs and chests, well-made with dovetails and mortice joints, the legs and feet carved to represent those of animals, the surfaces veneered and decorated with marquetry. The Greeks had lavishly decorated beds, used as couches in the daytime, standing on legs turned on the lathe. By adding a back and arms, the Romans provided the prototype for the classical, scroll-ended sofa, popular throughout Europe and America during the first half of the last century. Another Roman favourite was the *curule* – a stool with a type of X-shaped support that reappears, again and again, in successive periods. What has survived from the Romanesque period of the 13th century is of massive, if crude, construction, and some of it is painted in bright colours.

The Gothic Style

The true Gothic period flourished from about 1200–1600, and much later it enjoyed several revivals: 18th century *(Chippendale Gothic)*; early 19th *(Regency Gothic)*; late 19th *(Victorian Gothic)*. **5** Pointed arches, crocketed columns, foliage, the human face and figure – all may be found carved on furniture of the first period, but some is quite plain, relieved only with large, often decorative, strap-hinges and lock-plates of iron. An oak coffer of this description is the most likely find for the private collector looking for something as early as 1500. It will be of *plank construction*, that is boards joined together with iron nails or wooden pins. **6**

4 *Italian bronze dressing table and stool in the classical style, the kind of furniture used by the ancient Greeks and Romans and revived in the 18th century.*

5 *Book carrier with Gothic tracery and finials. English, the Victorian period.*

5

6 *Gothic oak chest of plank construction, with strap hinges and iron lock plate. English, late 15th century.*

6

7 *English oak coffer, with framed construction, circa 1600.*

7

8 *William and Mary highboy of walnut, veneered on white pine-mouldings. The base is of solid walnut. American (New England, circa 1710).*

9 *Armchair bearing the trade label of Giles Grendey, London, together with impressed workman's initials 'H W'. Japanned beech, with gilt decoration. Part of a very large suite made for the Duke of Infantado's castle at Lazcano in northern Spain, circa 1730.*

10 *English oak joined chair, with the linenfold motif on four of the panels and Renaissance ornamentation. 1525-50.*

A little later, framed construction became more general. Into a framework of narrow strips, panels were inserted, their edges made thin by chamfering so that they fitted into the rebate of the frame. **7** Hutches and what we call *cupboards* were made in this way, their panels often carved to represent scrolls of parchment – popularly known as *linenfold*.

The relatively few chairs made were throne-like, with high backs, box seats and enclosed arms. They were reserved for the use of important people, and to this day we preserve the tradition by asking a highly respected individual to *take the chair* at a meeting. **10** The less exalted sat on a stool or bench, in its Gothic form, slab-ended, with a strengthening piece placed on edge under the seat and projecting through the ends, where it was wedged into place.

Massive tables for communal meals, taken in the hall of the castle, were made to be taken apart easily, the movable tops being supported on heavy trestles. Such tables do appear on the market. The problem usually is deciding whether the top, often of elm, is the original one or a much later replacement. Solving it needs the help of a specialist in early furniture.

The Renaissance Style

Roman architecture began to be studied seriously again from about 1400, and in Italy, many pieces were made like miniature buildings, the woodwork painted or gilded and inlaid with coloured stones.

Again, the most important article was the chest – *cassone* – of sarcophagus shape with curving front and ends, made of walnut or cypress and carved in relief or painted – often by first-class artists – with representations of Christian saints or the gods and goddesses of Olympus.

Equipped with back and arms, the *cassone* became a monumental settle – *cassa panca* – but more comfortable seating was provided by folding chairs with the classical X-shaped frames – known as *Savonarola* chairs in Italy, and *Luther* in Germany.

The French interpreted Italian Renaissance ideas in their own way, during the reigns of François I and Henri II, which covered the greater part of the 16th century. Of particular interest are the *dressoir* (a cupboard resting on a stand) and the *armoire-à-deux-corps* (a two-part cupboard) which were richly carved with caryatids, half-human figures, as supports. Pieces of this kind, long out of fashion, are now (in the early 1970s) very much in demand and sell for high prices.

British craftsmen were influenced both directly and indirectly by the Renaissance. Italian woodworkers were brought to England by Henry VIII to practise their art on Hampton Court. By about 1550, quantities of furniture, mainly oak, were being imported from the Netherlands, some of it exhibiting Italian characteristics, especially in the carving, which was much more free in feeling than the traditional English Gothic.

In place of the communal board, came the domestic dining-table with draw-leaves sliding out from under the top and robustly-turned, melon-shaped legs. This type is still manufactured and can look very convincing with its *distressed* finish. Genuinely old oak tends to go dark right through its thickness, without artificial aids, and stain on the underneath of *anything* should always be regarded with suspicion.

Another favourite *Elizabethen* item is the four-poster bed, with posts which are elongated versions of the table-leg described above. In fact, there are very few beds old enough for it to be said of them 'Queen Elizabeth slept here'. With the introduction of the *farthingale* chairs, rather square in back and seat, which were upholstered, and without arms, ladies wearing wide, framed skirts could sit in comfort. Before 1600 such chairs were made singly or in pairs – not in sets.

The Jacobean style outlasted, by many years, the reign of James I, from whom it takes its name, being used to cover much of the period of Charles I and even the Commonwealth, although the term '*Cromwellian*' is sometimes used to describe certain things of the 1650s, such as chairs rather like the farthingale type, but covered in leather and made in sets, and the early versions of the gate-leg table. **11** In country districts in Britain, and in America, the style continued popular until 1700, and even later.

When the Pilgrim Fathers arrived in America in 1620, they brought little furniture with them, and had to make their own. Most of the early settlers were English by origin, with a sprinkling of Dutch, Swedish, German and Spanish. Their furniture was therefore based largely on English models, with some Continental influences and, most important, a very strong, local

11 *English oak top table on three turned legs with fold-down flap, 17th century.*

individuality that the expert can recognize.

The lathe was employed to produce legs for chairs and tables in a wide variety of baluster forms; flat, frontal surfaces were often decorated with *split turnery* by taking two lengths of wood which were lightly glued together, turned on the lathe as one piece and divided again by splitting the temporary joint, so that the flat side of each piece could then be glued and pinned as a decoration to the front of a chest or cupboard.

Mouldings arranged geometrically provided a favourite way of decorating chests-of-drawers, which evolved fairly early in the 17th century, from the coffer. Beginning as a box with a lid, it was first fitted with one or two drawers at the bottom, the rest of the space remaining in box form. The fronts of such chests were often decorated with mouldings to simulate more drawer-fronts in addition to the real ones. Such hybrids are popularly known as *mule chests*. Gradually more and more chests were made with practical drawers throughout.

In unsophisticated areas the coffer-type of chest persisted, and there is a well-known range of early American specimens with distinctive qualities. One of the earliest-known makers was Nicholas Disbrowe (1612-83), born in Essex, England, who settled in Hartford, Connecticut. A chest bearing his signature is carved all over the front with a tulip design. This method of covering the entire front of a chest with flat carving was practised also by John Allis and Samuel Belding, of Hadley and Hatfield on the Connecticut River, 1675-1740, and by Thomas Dennis in Ipswich, Massachusetts. A number of pieces attributed to the latter are in the Museum of Fine Arts, Boston. They are mainly of oak, with elm, ash and poplar as secondary woods for drawer-linings and backs, and are carved with flat *strapwork*.

Yet another recognizable New England type is the Connecticut *tulip and sunflower* chest, which always has these flowers carved in low relief, in the panels only, the framework being left plain. Here, the treatment is reminiscent of Dutch furniture. This must not be confused with *Pennsylvania Dutch* – a misnomer, the word being a corruption of *Deutsch*. This furniture was made by settlers of German origin, and was cheerfully painted in bright colours.

Chairs, both with and without arms, became much more general during the 17th century. Some were upholstered, but many were entirely of wood, or wood with rush seats. Spindle-backs were popular in England and America, and are often a triumph of the wood-turner's art. The American versions tend to be rather Dutch in feeling, the front legs being heavy posts which extend upwards to support the arms. Two traditional types are the *Carver* – with a single row of spindles in the back – and the *Brewster* – with two rows – each named after the Pilgrim Father said to have introduced its prototype to America.

The press cupboard was also common to both Britain and America. It had its origins in the Elizabethan court cupboard, literally a 'cup board'. In the Jacobean period, first one space between the tiers, then the other, became either wholly or partly enclosed with panels and doors, leading to the creation of a 'cupboard' as we understand the term today. As a type, the press cupboard survived longest in Wales, where it continued to be made until the late 18th century.

Mention of Wales leads naturally to the dresser which started life in the Jacobean period as a side-table standing on turned legs, with drawers – usually three – set side by side in the frieze. There was no rack of shelves *attached* to it, but with the fashion for Delft pottery that developed in Britain in the late 17th century, a rack for its display was often set on the wall *above* the dresser. Eventually, dressers came to be made complete with racks. What is known as a *Welsh dresser* was not originally peculiar to Wales, but did enjoy so much popularity there that distinctive types emerged: South Wales – fitted with drawers below and an open pot-board; 13 West Wales – three drawers, two cupboards with space between *(dog kennel)*; North Wales – base completely enclosed with cupboards and drawers. These do not belong to the Jacobean period, but they are in the tradition of country-made furniture that owes much to it.

The Baroque Style

Baroque means, literally, 'irregular pearl' and, considered as artistry, it was just that – an essential beauty, strangely and grotesquely exaggerated. Beginning in Italy towards the end of the Renaissance, it contrived to use many materials and a multiplicity of shapes. Typical forms were 'S'-shaped, hook-like curves; decoration included cherubs clambering among swags of fruit around shields and scrolls, spiral columns, grinning

satyrs, negro slaves supporting cabinets, and Greek goddesses surmounting the cornices. **15** All this was brought under control, in the second half of the 17th century, by the brilliant team who worked in France to create the Palace of Versailles for Louis XIV. Techniques long forgotten were re-discovered – marquetry, parquetry and the use of veneers among them.

Veneering is the process of overlaying a foundation of solid timber, often oak or pine, with a relatively thin sheet of finely figured wood. Economy apart, effects can be achieved in this way which are impossible with solid wood. Marquetry is the inlaying of a design, using a variety of veneers, into a groundwork of veneer. Parquetry is the formation of a geometrical pattern by setting small squares of veneer against each other, so that their contrasting colours and opposing grains create the optical illusion of a three-dimensional effect.

A highly specialized form of marquetry was that perfected by the cabinet-maker Boulle (or Buhl), who covered large surfaces with a veneer of tortoiseshell, laid over coloured micre, and inlaid it with intricate designs – *arabesques* – cut out of thin brass. This technique was revived at intervals, notably in England during the Regency period (1800-30) and again, in both France and England, about 1860. Most of the Boulle furniture seen on the market today is of this last period.

The Baroque arrived a little belatedly in England, which had been torn by civil war and repressed by the ensuing Commonwealth and Protectorate under Oliver Cromwell. But when the monarchy was restored in 1660, Charles II brought with him from exile on the Continent the latest ideas of comfort and elegance. The highly-skilled cabinet-maker now began to use veneers, and marquetry with either bold, floral designs or intricate patterns known as *seaweed* in light-coloured woods on a dark ground, such as ebony.

Chairs were tall, with arched backs, and narrow caned seats. The cresting-rail at the top of the back and the stretcher joining the front legs were ornately carved, a popular device being two cherubs supporting a crown. **17** Legs were turned to a baluster shape or a spiral – the *barley-sugar* twist. Arm-chairs were similar, but wider in the seat, the arms being scrolled downwards at the front. Some were richly upholstered in Genoa velvets, at enormous expense, the material having to be imported. Only the very rich could afford a settee or a day-bed, made on the lines of the caned chairs, with adjustable head-rest. This article, and chairs in the Charles II style were also made in America, but not in large numbers.

Most significant in England, was the change in fashion from oak to walnut, used both in the solid and in veneers, and supplemented by laburnum, olive, ebony and a variety of other woods for marquetry. **16** Another novelty was the lacquer-work imported by the East India Companies into Europe from China and Japan. **14** These cabinets, mounted on carved and gilded stands were soon being imitated in most European countries,

13

the art of *japanning* being practised by both professional and amateur. **9** This craze reached America about 1700, and japanned furniture, with quaint local characteristics, was produced commercially in Boston from then until the outbreak of the Revolution.

Between 1685 and 1700 thousands of French Protestants – Huguenots – fled from France to find refuge in Holland and Britain. Many were craftsmen in furniture, textiles and silver. Daniel Marôt, a highly gifted cabinet-maker and designer went to Holland, to find employment with William of Orange who in 1689, with his English wife, Mary, ascended the English throne. **18** As a result of all this England absorbed a great many French and Dutch ideas during the last fifteen years of the 17th century.

Perhaps the most significant developments were

14

15

14 *Bantam work incised lacquer cabinet on giltwood stand against a tapestry background.*

15 *Florentine Pietra Dura cabinet, decorated with flowers and birds, Italian, 17th century (the stand is early 19th century).*

16 *English 'oyster' walnut and yew tree marquetry chest-of-drawers, circa 1685.*

the setting-up of a textile industry capable of producing upholstery materials; great improvements in the quality and size of mirror-plates, and the discarding of the twist leg in favour of a simple turned one. Chair legs were made with a pronounced inverted cup towards the top, a tapering shaft and a bold *bun* foot. Then a leg following an 'S'-shaped curve emerged, shortly to be smoothed out and become the *cabriole*. The tops of cabinets were shaped into double domes.

In America the William and Mary style continued long after William's death in 1702. It is particularly agreeable, being lighter and less flamboyant than its Anglo-Dutch counterparts. Popular items were the chest-on-stand *(highboy)* – essentially a chest-of-drawers raised on legs; **8** the bureau-bookcase *(secretary-desk)* with mirrored doors; winged arm-chairs; grate-leg tables with oval tops and turned legs, of which one type – the *butterfly* table, so-called because of the wing-shaped supports for its leaves – seems to have originated in New England.

Walnut was used in Pennsylvania, but in the North Eastern areas it was less readily available and maple, assisted with pine, predominated. In New York, there was a strong Dutch tradition that lasted at least until the early 19th century, which favoured a massive cupboard – *kas* – made of fruitwood and painted with swags of fruit.

From the late 17th century onwards, many of the most characteristic English and American articles of furniture were constructed in two separate stages, the upper simply resting on the lower. The *highboy*, the *secretary desk* and the cabinet-on-stand, with two doors enclosing an elaborate fitment of little drawers, are good examples. Often pieces are found with both top and bottom basically genuine but which do not belong to each other. Signs of trimming to achieve a reasonably good fit should be looked out for; the outside of the backs should be compared to see if they are of the same wood; inconsistency in veneers, and especially in any cross-banding, herringbone, or *stringing* (thin lines of wood inlaid into the surface) is highly suspicious.

Walnut continued to be the most fashionable wood in England during the reign of Anne (1702-14), when native craftsmen anglicized the Continental influences of the preceding forty years. The cabriole leg was fully developed into a gracious curve, echoed in the swan's neck shaping of the chair-back around the vase-shaped splat. Marquetry was rather less in favour, interest being concentrated on beautifully figured wood. Carving was generally confined to a detail – the shell on the knee of a leg or, from about 1710, a claw-and-ball foot.

The kneehole dressing-table, with its arrangement of small drawers embracing a small cupboard recessed in the kneehole, is an article that always needs looking at closely, to ensure that it has not been converted from a genuine, but less important, chest-of-drawers. Always turn it upside-down and study the construction below,

16

where signs of alteration are most easily seen.

American furniture in the Queen Anne style also shook off the influence of the New York Dutch. Though tending to be later in date than its English models, it follows them fairly closely in design, with some local variations in detail. During the first half of the 18th century, there were three main centres of furniture-making in America – Philadelphia, Boston and Newport, Rhode Island. Job Townsend of Newport is credited with the introduction of a motif regarded as essentially American – a concave shell carved in the apron below the central bottom drawer in both the highboy and the lowboy. **21**

In England and America throughout the 18th century, handles were of brass, at least on sophisticated furniture. Original brasswork is always rightly claimed as an enhancement, but an otherwise attractive article

should not be rejected merely because the handles have been replaced, nor should preoccupations with the finer furniture preclude an interest in the simple country styles. The rush-seated chair with *ladder* or *splat* back was usually made of ash or beech in England, and of maple in the Delaware River Valley. Ultimately, the city copies its country cousins, fine ladder-back chairs of mahogany being made in the 1750s and 1760s.

The Rococo Style

During the Queen Anne period, English and American furniture grew more feminine. During that of George I (1714-27), there was a masculine reaction led by the architect William Kent, who borrowed heavily from the Palladian style and made some extravagant ventures into the Baroque; but his work was limited to commissions for great houses.

17 *William and Mary chair, carved in walnut in the manner of Daniel Marôt. English, circa 1696.*

18 *Charles II chair, believed to have been owned by Nell Gwynne. The cresting and stretcher are carved with crowned bust supported by amorini.*

17

18

France remained under the rule of Louis XIV until 1715, when he was succeeded by his great-grandson, Louis XV. For eight years, while the new king was still a minor, his uncle, Philip, Duke of Orléans, acted as regent. The *Régence* is important because of its reaction against the heavy Versailles style, the leader of the artistic revolution being Charles Cressent, cabinet-maker to Philip. He developed curvilinear shapes for carcasses – notably the *commode* with *bombé* front and ends – and extended the use of ormolu (gilded bronze) mounts. **3** The effect is still rather heavy, but the serpentine curves suggest a feminine quality which was to blossom into the Rococo style of Louis XV – *rocaille*, meaning *rock and shell work*.

Rocks and shells are, indeed, sometimes present. So are flowers and foliage, bows of ribbon and absurd *chinoiseries* – a traveller's tale Orient. Straight lines were never used if it was at all possible to employ a curve. Surfaces were veneered in exotic woods, the frames of seat-furniture were either painted, gilt or left the natural colour of the solid wood. Table legs were veneered but *not* chair legs, until revivals in the 19th century.

These Victorian copies of French furniture of the great periods are frequently of fine quality. The originals are normally beyond the reach of the modest purse, especially if signed by their makers, most of whom belonged to a guild which required them to stamp their names on their products. **22** Some of the finest craftsmen, however, were excused from this obligation – particularly foreign immigrants. The French Rococo was the creation of an international brigade of talent, but many of the best makers were French by birth – like Leleu, who trained under the mighty Oeben and hoped

19 *Carved giltwood arm-chair, French, circa 1775. Properly this is a* bergère *in the French sense, that is an arm-chair with cushions and enclosed arms as distinct from a* fauteuil *which has open arms and no cushion on the seat. In England the term 'bergère' is traditionally applied to a chair with caned arms and back.*

20 *Chippendale walnut chair made in Philadelphia, circa 1760.*

19

20

to take over his business one day; but the Widow Oeben took a fancy instead to Riesener, one of the German immigrants.

These inventive craftsmen made a remarkable variety of tables and desks, chairs and settees, and superb *commodes* (chests-of-drawers). Flowers and landscapes were depicted in marquetry; *fêtes galantes* scenes, in the style of Watteau, Boucher and Fragonard were painted on panels and treated with a special varnish invented by two brothers called Martin, so that the whole technique has come to be known as *Vernis Martin*.

English Rococo, and the closely-related American, is generally more sober than the French, although its best-known practitioner, Thomas Chippendale, included some very frivolous designs among those he first published in 1754, in a book entitled *The Gentleman and the Cabinet Maker's Director*. **23** The several styles associated with his name are clearly seen in the chairs of the period. There is the well-known type with fretted centre-splat, reaching its most extreme elaboration in the *ribbon-back* and standing on cabriole legs that terminated in feet carved to an up-turned scroll, in the French manner, or resembling an animal's foot – claw-and-ball, or lion's paw. Reproductions of such chairs abound. A really fine, genuine set is hard to find and likely to be highly priced, so beware of 'bargains'.

Chinese Chippendale is a term applied to chairs on square legs with backs and arms latticed like the windows of a Chinese house. A much more extreme excursion into *chinoiserie* is seen in carved and gilt mirrors with little figures of mandarins, dragons, exotic birds and pagodas. The pagoda type of roof was also used for bookcases and cabinets.

21

22

21 *Queen Anne walnut highboy and matching lowboy, Salem, Massachusetts, USA, circa 1750-69.*

22 *The name of a French cabinet-maker – Lardin, who became a master in 1750 – stamped into the wood of one of his products, as required by his guild and by law. Such stamps are usually tucked away discreetly on an inconspicuous part of the framework – in this case, on the top of the commode, concealed by the marble.*

Chippendale Gothic employed such features as rose windows, cluster-columns and the pointed arch; but there was no attempt to pass anything off as medieval, other than in style. Oak, the true Gothic material, was seldom used. The fashionable wood was mahogany which had begun to come in from Cuba and the Honduras about 1720, and remained the most popular wood for at least half a century until the advent of satinwood, and even then it never really went out of favour.

The Chippendale style arrived in America about 1760 and became immensely popular. All, or nearly all the English mannerisms were adopted, but block-fronted chests-of-drawers owe more to Germanic influence. John Goddard of Newport specialized in these pieces, decorating them with a carved shell motif of a particularly large size. In Philadelphia, William Savery was one of those who produced fine pieces in the Chippendale style, while Thomas Affleck and Benjamin Randolph were especially adept at the Rococo manner, remaining devoted to the claw-and-ball foot. The style continued popular at least until 1785. **20** Specialized knowledge is needed to recognize the most subtle differences between English and American Chippendale – American chairs, for example, tending to be slightly narrower in the seat than English ones.

The Neo-Classic Style

While the Rococo retained its popularity in America until long after the War of Independence, it had already begun to lose its appeal in France by 1755, and in England by 1760. The answer was a return to discipline – to straight lines, ovals and circles in place of S-shaped curves and C-scrolls. Excavations of Roman sites at Pompeii and Herculaneum sparked off enthusiasm for the classical column, the urn, the ram's head, the trophy of arms, the classically draped figure and the rest of the repertoire of ornament associated with the style of Adam in Britain, and with that called *Louis XVI* in France, although it was, in fact, well established before he came to the throne in 1774. **12**

There was a transitional phase between the Rococo and the Neo-Classic, during which ornament led the way, and shapes of furniture followed more slowly, the cabriole leg eventually being replaced by a vertical one. Another form of enrichment which remained popular during the Louis XVI period was the use of porcelain plaques made at the royal factory at Sèvres.

Most of the old favourites survived in modified form: the *bureau plat* (flat-topped writing table); the *bonheur-du-jour* (a lady's desk, with a small superstructure); the *bergère* (arm-chair with padded back, enclosed arms, cushioned seat); **19** and the *fauteuil* (arm-chair, padded back, open arms, no cushion). One of the daughters of Louis XV remarked that it was only her cosy *bergère* that stopped her entering a convent.

In Britain, Robert Adam led the classical revival in design after returning from a Continental tour in 1758. He was the architect to whom most English furniture of the later 18th century owes something. At its most effective, it is decorated with urns, rams' heads, Corinthian columns; but there is a diluted version for modest homes.

Into this middle range come the plain but good pieces of mahogany, chest-of-drawers, Pembroke tables with small flaps, toilet mirrors of oval or shield shape, sideboards and chairs on square, tapered legs, gentlemen's wardrobes with cupboards above and drawers below – *brown* furniture, as it is called, a little disparagingly, by those who prefer the more richly decorated pieces – the painted satinwood in the style of Angelica Kauffmann, the carved and gilt seat-furniture, the marquetry-decorated, semi-elliptical commodes of the 1770s and 1780s. But the simple mahogany furniture remains, for most people of modest means, a very good buy. **26**

Hepplewhite's designs were published in 1788, two years after his death, by his widow, Alice. Most of the legs he illustrated for tables and chairs were vertical, either square-tapered or delicately turned and fluted; but he retained an elegant form of the cabriole for pieces in the style known as *French Hepplewhite*. **27** Chair-backs were mostly oval, shield- or heart-shaped, but some were square. The characteristic carving of pendant husks, bell-flowers, wheat-sheaves and the Prince of Wales' feathers is refined and unassertive on good Hepplewhite furniture.

George Hepplewhite may well have been the inventor of the sideboard as one piece of furniture with cupboards and drawers, standing on tapered legs, as distinct from the earlier combination of serving table flanked by a pair of free-standing cupboards supporting urns. American sideboards in the Hepplewhite style have some distinctive features. Though elegantly serpentine-fronted, the ornamentation is usually very simple, being restricted to *stringing* in satinwood or maple. The knee-hole-like cavity that occurs at the centre of many English specimens is more often occupied by a drawer in the American version.

The more obvious influences of Robert Adam are

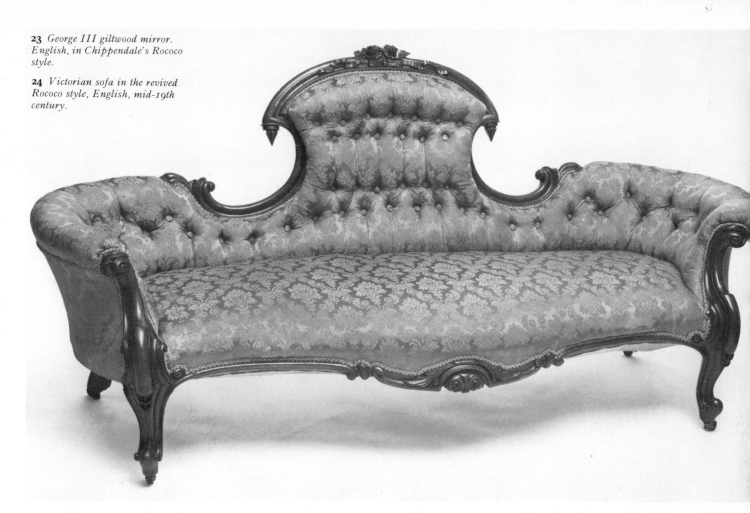

23 *George III giltwood mirror. English, in Chippendale's Rococo style.*

24 *Victorian sofa in the revived Rococo style, English, mid-19th century.*

largely absent from American furniture. His designs were not published there, and the outbreak of the Revolution in 1765 inevitably delayed the arrival of Neo-Classicism, until it had already mellowed into the less self-assertive manner of Hepplewhite and Sheraton.

Thomas Sheraton was a cabinet-maker by trade, who came to London and set up as drawing master in Soho. There is no known piece of furniture that can be attributed to his hand. (Unlike so much of the French, English furniture of the 18th century is seldom signed.) His designs were first published in 1791, and reflect the taste of his day, although it is often difficult, especially with American furniture, to say whether a particular piece owes more to the influence of Hepplewhite or Sheraton. John Seymour of Boston, Samuel McIntire of Salem, and Matthew Egerton of New Jersey were prominent among the American interpreters of this style, known as *Federal*.

The Empire Style

Following the French Revolution, there was a powerful reaction against the luxurious trappings of the monarchy. Some of the Parisian cabinet-makers survived to make much more severe furniture, still in the Neo-Classic style but without too many enrichments, over a short period known as *Directoire*. A more scholastic approach to Ancient Rome, Greece and Egypt resulted in chairs with sabre legs, couches with turned feet and scrolled ends, tables supported by sphinx-like figures. This pattern was aggrandized to glorify the Empire (1804-15) under Napoleon, when a vast amount of furniture was made, some 10,000 workmen being employed in Paris.

A similar fashion prevailed in England, where the style is known as *English Empire* or *Regency*, and lasted from about 1800 to 1830. Led by designers Henry Holland and Thomas Hope, and popularized by practical cabinet-makers such as George Smith, it was a little less grand than the French version, but nevertheless produced some handsome and even ornate furniture. Characteristic pieces are sofa-tables, with short flaps at the ends; circular tables on centre-columns of pyramid shape; chairs with sabre or turned legs; and dwarf bookcases with *grille* doors which were formed of a brass mesh, backed with silk. Brass was extensively used for intricate inlay-work on a ground of rosewood or mahogany.

In America, there was a conscious attempt, sponsored by Jefferson, to follow the French rather than the English model at this time, and to some extent this succeeded by virtue of an influx of French craftsmen into New York, who were familiar with the Empire style; but the best-known American maker of the period was already established there – Duncan Phyfe, a Scot by birth, who was active from about 1795 to 1847. One of his favourite forms was the X-shaped base for chairs and tables, and his Grecian-style sofas set a fashion which was long-lived.

The Victorian Style

The Victorians revived practically every known style – Gothic, Renaissance, Baroque, Rococo, Neo-Classical – and managed to impart to each a flavour all their own. True, they made things which loudly proclaimed their 19th-century self-confidence, but some of the drawing-room furniture is charming. **24** In New York City, John Belter produced centre-tables and

25

26

27

25 *A typical Shaker room, showing drop-leaf table, armed rocking chair, chest of drawers with drop-leaf top of lightly stained maple, and panelled window casing painted 'heavenly blue'.*

26 *George III mahogany-framed chair, English, in the French Hepplewhite style.*

27 *Mahogany secrétaire chest, attributed to Chippendale, Haig and Company. Third quarter of the 18th century.*

28 *Regency Cabinet with brass inlay, marble top and glazed doors lined with pleated silk.*

console-tables with marble tops mounted on stands so burdened with bunches of fruit and flowers that the cabriole legs seem to be bending under the strain.

After 1860, there was a reaction against the excesses of Victorianism, led by William Morris and the Pre-Raphaelites in Britain, and by Charles Eastlake in America. Their ideas were based on a rejection of the machine and a romantic return to medievalism, but this was soon, in its turn, to be commercialized. Finally, at the end of the 19th century, came *Art Nouveau*, which combined the severity of the British Arts and Crafts Movement with the Continental *whiplash line*.

There was also the pleasant cottage furniture which continued well into the 19th century, in both Britain and America; the chaste furniture made by the American religious sect, the *Shakers*, is typical and did not even have a brass handle to brighten it. **25**

SILVER

At the beginning of the 20th century any silver lacking the pedigree of good English hallmarks would be found lurking at the back of American closets, for the true merit of Colonial silver was still unrecognized in the States and unseen by the rest of the world. It was not that these marks had much meaning; it was more that they proclaimed the plate to be English, or Scottish, or Irish, and therefore desirable. Few marks had been deciphered at the time, for the English hallmarking system was never intended as a code to be read by all, but as an aid to the maintenance of law within the goldsmith's craft. This has proved to be of advantage to the English, for the story those marks are able to tell increases interest in the silver itself.

American silver is still too scarce in Europe for any idea of its characteristics to be formed, and those crossing the Atlantic to see it for the first time are liable to be surprised. They must be forgiven if they expect to find a simplified version of English silver, somewhat behind the times, for American writers have been apt to describe it that way, sometimes with justification. It is true, for instance, that most of it was made for use in the home, the same vessels to be taken to church when needed. Thus the greater extravagances of English and Continental sculptural goldsmiths were out of place, although most major museums are able to display examples of such intricate craftsmanship. Looking at museum silver is a part of our education, since studying the best examples helps wise buying.

The earliest American craftsmen were London trained, but as they had crossed the Atlantic to escape English restrictions, they desired no guilds for the protection of their work such as they had in England. In London the Worshipful Company of Goldsmiths, who had been given a Royal Charter in 1327, stamped the mark of the leopard's head on silver they had tested and proved to be of sterling standard, so that they could punish the maker (known after 1363 by his own mark, stamped alongside the leopard's head) if his work was unsatisfactory. In Boston, Robert Sanderson (1608-93) gladly punched his personal mark but it was the boast of American goldsmiths that they needed no supervision and even the word *sterling* was not stamped on their silver until after 1850, when it had largely ceased to be hand-made anyway.

The sterling standard, 92.5 % pure silver to 7.5 % copper, was first perfected in Germany many centuries before being adopted in England, where no lesser standard was ever used legally. The finest Continental silver was also of this standard, but as each silver-making centre was independently ruled, no standards were invariable in any given country. English silver coins had also been of the sterling standard and it was probably because this was debased that Goldsmith's Hall introduced the mark of the *lion passant* in 1544, to show invariable quality. With the date letter, which appeared officially in 1478, this made a total of four marks on London Plate and, like the maker's mark, was probably copied from Montpelier in France, who had already used it. By the date letter the warden responsible would be known if a hallmarked item was later found to be below standard, as such men were not above accepting bribes.

Although more than 150 silversmiths were recorded in Boston alone before 1800, this problem did not arise and Sanderson, his partner John Hull (1624-83) and other immigrants, fired by enthusiasm for the new, free life, made high quality silver and trained others to keep up these standards. The goldsmiths of New York set up their workshops about a generation later, men with Dutch names who made silver in the Dutch style, although under English rule, while the first of Philadelphia's craftsmen appeared in the 1690s, making silver for wealthy Quakers who required quality without frills. Canada's first goldsmiths also started work in the late 17th century, almost entirely in Quebec and Montreal. They worked largely for the Church and the designs were very French in concept.

The American porringer was the first distinctively trans-Atlantic item of silver to be made that had no real English equivalent. These medium-sized, flat, shallow bowls, with a single pierced handle, were found in quantity in almost every New England home and were

entirely domestic in use. **30** Piercing on the handles, which also had initials engraved, were at first a subject of much variety, although later it became almost universally *keyhole*. In New York, where fewer porringers were made, piercing was often so intricate that no space remained for initials, a loss to the silver historian, for tracing the family tree connected with initials in America replaced the interest hallmarks bestowed in England.

In the last half of the 17th century the English made two-handled cups of German derivation, also known as porringers or sometimes caudle cups, the name given to the simplified form made in America. **31** There they were never larger than one person could hold comfortably, but in England these richly embossed bowls varied in size from being quite small to being large enough to hold a gallon or more. They were usually gourd-shaped, as in Germany, with caryatid handles, but sometimes sloped gently from a rounded base, when they might have simple scroll handles instead, and a nicely rounded, well-fitting lid, which was embossed like the bowl, but which has not always survived. Their purpose was to keep the spiced wine or 'caudle' hot while people prepared for the night in freezing bedrooms. The caudle was ladled out into the smaller cups from the enormous communal pot which was brought in with the individual night candles. No doubt their use was much the same in the States, where some cups were gourd shaped, like the English, only taller and usually plain with simple 'S'-scroll handles and initials. Generalization is apt to throw up exceptions, however, and Benjamin Sanderson (1649-78), son of Robert, produced a nicely decorated cup only just over two inches high, while another, five and a half inches high, by Gerrit Oncklebag (1670-1732) of New York, has attractive beaded caryatid handles and a plain body.

These cups draw attention to another, extraordinarily attractive, New York two-handled bowl, made in the 17th and 18th centuries. It was developed from the Dutch brandy bowl used for holding raisins soaked in brandy which were eaten straight from the bowl with silver spoons on special, family occasions. In New York they were oval, as in Holland after 1670, and shallow in proportion to width, and often commemorated a marriage. They were incised with deep lines, forming six sections, in which nicely curved panels enclose embossed, or sometimes engraved floral decoration. Caryatid handles are the rule and some also have a surprise on the base, an additional decoration to be examined when the bowl is empty.

Candles must have been as important to life in America as elsewhere, but very few holders survive in silver, one exception being a pair in the French clustered-column style, engraved 1686, by Jeremiah Dummer (1645-1718), the first American-born silversmith in Boston. Holders were also comparatively rare in England before 1700, when they were gloriously simple, but examples after that date are collectors' favourites, and have remained popular and expensive, particularly those made all through the 18th century by the great Huguenot craftsmen. **32**

It was not until the city of Sheffield started specializing in holders in 1773 that they became easier on the purse. They are stamped on the base with hallmarks that include the extra punch of a crown, denoting silver made in Sheffield, and after 1784 the sovereign's head was stamped on all English silver to show a duty paid. The smiths of an industrial city like Sheffield were determined to cut costs by mechanizing the craft, while

31 *Charles II porringer and cover, maker's mark 'TH' or 'IH', circa 1665. This type of lid finial was used as a base when reversed to serve as a dish.*

32 *Exceptionally fine half of a pair of George III two-light candelabra. Prices run very high for such a standard of line and workmanship. London made.*

still producing the latest styles. They used such thin machine-rolled silver that the sticks required leading to hold their shape. These methods continued to evolve so that Sheffield-made candlesticks are always cheaper than those of London, but are also renowned for variety and quality of design.

Church plate was made in Britain and America, but at the time that the old Mass chalices were replaced by new communion cups in England, mostly between about 1565 and 1580, the ancestors of those who founded the New World were kneeling in the churches of English villages and towns. Many of those lovely cups survive, but the colonists who went to Massachusetts had more in common with the Scottish kirk, which allowed vessels to be used in the home and taken to church on Sundays. Of these the beaker, used all over the north of Scotland, was the most popular in Boston, a very early example having been made by Sanderson and Hull, both of whom had been dead many years before 1728 when it was donated to the First Church of Christ in Marblehead, for its use alone. Six inches high, it is straight-sided, flaring only slightly at the lip, set on a convex foot with a nicely moulded edge and decorated with interlacing strapwork near the top, supporting a pendant of floral design.

Both in shape and decoration this beaker is very like the Dutch beakers so popular in the Scottish kirk, which were taken to Aberdeen originally by students from Leyden University in Holland. They were copied by the Scots profusely and later simplified, but were always more interesting than those made in London or Norwich, which also had close connections with the Dutch. The form in New England soon changed, becoming very varied, but more than a century later the link with Aberdeen was further strengthened when the first bishop of America was consecrated there in 1784, London having refused to help out a rebel.

The tankard was another secular drinking vessel taken to church in America, a use that could never have been contemplated in England where it was too well imbued with the convivial spirit. **36, 37** Often very large, holding several pints, it was originally used for communal drinking, which sometimes led to fighting. The Scandinavians had the answer to this with their peg tankard designed to keep any one man from taking more than his share by the insertion of a measured row of pegs down the inside. From about 1650 these were squat and drum-shaped, raised on three feet of the ball and claw design, or in the shape of a pomegranate, or even a lion, with the thumbpiece frequently matching. Sometimes they had a coin inserted in the lid, as those from

New York did later on. **38** In the last quarter of the century, cut card work appeared on the body at the junction with the feet, strengthening the silver. In America only two peg tankards were made, by two of the greatest craftsmen, John Coney of Boston (1656-1722) and Cornelius Kierstede of New York (1675-1757), but in England they were made in considerable numbers in the north, in very much the same form as the Scandinavian ones, but without the coin. **37**

The everyday English tankard at the time was still inclined to be large and, until about 1700, drum-shaped, a little taller in proportion to width than the very squat Scandinavian type, with a flat stepped lid, a beautifully engraved coat of arms on the body and a fine thumbpiece. One of the most effective of these is a *lion couchant*, sprawling lazily across and onto the lid, and very occasionally the bowl is also supported on three lion feet, such as John Coney used for his famous triangular standish.

The American tankard was small by comparison, rarely holding more than a pint, and was often soberly inscribed on the handle with the initials of both husband and wife. In basic shape it evolved less than in England, where date can be told at a glance by lid and body features, and it continued with the flat top much longer. The domed lid, which in England was normal from about 1710 onwards, appeared more consistently in Philadelphia, but when used in Boston it was also surmounted by a moulded finial for a while. Paul Revere (1735-1818) made several of these in his early period, with an interesting cast finial, the round body broken by a raised rib, as in England. Arms were also engraved quite frequently, in both Boston and Philadelphia.

Despite these English points the American tankard was altogether distinctive, one positive feature being the shield at the tip of the handle, in varying shapes, usually bearing an applied mask that was totally individual. In addition there was a beaded drop, or a rat-tail down the handle from the hinge, which might also have cut card or other decoration on it. The thumbpiece was usually scroll, or corkscrew in New York, only occasionally becoming more ambitious, as, for instance, Coney's eagle, or Timothy Dwight's (1654-91) lion. Dwight's tankard also has an unusual acanthus band around the bowl. The majority have a flanged lid, serrated in front, as another distinguishing feature.

In New York the general form was English, the Dutch never having made tankards, and the occasional use of coins in the lid came from Germany, yet their tankards are unmistakably New York, largely because of the variety of stamped narrow bands of decoration immediately above the moulded base of the drum-shaped body, often incorporating an interesting meander wire. In the early days some of these features were also used, in a simplified form, in Philadelphia, where tankards were notable for generous size, yet there is no confusing them with those of New York.

It is said that the collector's period in England started in 1660 when the Civil War was over and demands that plate be converted to coin gave way to an exuberance of richly decorated silver, Dutch and German in concept, in a gay and carefree age. However in 1697 the Britannia standard was introduced, raising the proportion of silver in the alloy used above that of sterling, making the metal too soft for such decoration. A period of superlative work in heavy gauge silver

followed, which was domestic in character with lovely lines and a rich, glowing patina. The designs were influenced overwhelmingly by the first Huguenots to arrive from France, the forerunners of men like Paul de Lamerie who took the craft through the Rococo period and were working at its height (1705-51). The sterling standard returned at the option of the maker in 1719 but for the majority the collector's period could not really be said to start until mechanized mills produced thin rolled silver in about 1770, and the Neo-Classic period began.

In America the war that cooled the melting pots did not take place before 1775, and even then their own Civil War (1861-5) was to come, with a demand on silver plate that amounted to extinction in the south, where goldsmiths had been strongly active. Nevertheless good domestic silver was made in all the American centres throughout the 18th century, largely to private order, as it always had been, because silver itself was scarce and used largely for important family occasions, permanently recorded by the engraving of initials and inscriptions. Styles became increasingly English, concentrating more upon workmanship and line than the latest fashion, spurning decoration beyond the use of gadroons or cut card applications in limited amounts, with armorials engraved on plain surfaces. After independence was gained in 1781 such anglicisms were frowned on, but the empty space looked so bare that initials were often dressed up to give the same impression. Even New York changed to English styles when Simeon Soumaine (1685-1750) arrived from London, although he cannot be held entirely responsible for this. His silver was quite plain, but Daniel Christian

Fueter from London (working in New York 1754-70) had a true understanding of Rococo, rare in America, which he displayed well on a pierced elliptical basket, with a cast applied rim. Even finer was the work of Joseph Richardson (1711-84) of Philadelphia, whose tea kettle on a stand was in high Rococo, beautifully executed, as were his richly decorated coffee pot and matching sugar bowl.

Chocolate pots, with their removable finial to allow the insertion of a stirring rod, and coffee pots were well made and differed from the English only in size and date. The octagonal form, used extensively in England early in the century, never seems to have found favour in America. Teapots in England were bullet-shaped from about 1720, but in America they remained high and pear-shaped, although Boston frequently made them in

35

33 *Selection of American cans and a creamer showing how initials were dressed up to look like armorials after Independence was gained.*

34 *Highly important pair of George II Baluster covered beer jugs, by Philippe Garden, 1754, sold by Sotheby's in 1969 for £17,000 ($44,200).*

35 *Silver chalice and paten dated 1518 that passed from the Church to the Bedingfield family.*

36 Tankard by Samuel Edwards of Boston, USA, 1759. The finial on the domed lid was a Boston feature.

37 English Provincial Peg tankard, by John Plummer, York, circa 1695.

38 New York tankard, circa 1730, probably by John Moulinar. This cylindrical tankard, with its James II coin inserted in the lid, incorporates all the features that distinguish New York tankards, except that the shield at the tip of the handle has no mask applied.

39 A George II tea kettle stand and lamp, by William Kidney 1739, an early example of the inverted pear shape. Decoration, unfortunately, tended to become more elaborate with time.

37

34

38

40 One of the highly important pair of Dutch wall sconces by Adam van Vianen, of Utrecht, dated 1622. Sold at Sotheby's in 1971 for £62,000 ($161,200). Adam van Vianen, born 1565, was the brother of the famous Paulus and father of Christiaen who made much royal plate for Charles I. The Dutch style in New York did not copy the work of such men.

41 Highly important pair of Elizabeth I parcel-gilt livery pots, maker's mark 'HL', date 1591.

42 Silver waiter with pierced rim and beaded edge, armorials filling the centre, as made in Philadelphia in the late-18th century.

42

43 the attractive inverted pear form, set on a splayed foot
with a cast finial surmounting a domed lid and beautifully decorated shoulders. As a group they are quite
outstanding and very popular now, although rare in
England.

The Greek revival, which in England began in 1770,
43 was delayed in America by the Revolution, but was
then equally popular. Any form of domestic hollow-
ware, whether cylindrical or urn-shaped, was suitable
for light, symmetrical decoration, piercing or bright
cut engraving, and Boston teapots sometimes also had
fluted drums, to lovely effect, particularly in the hands
of Paul Revere. In Philadelphia beading was very
frequently used around the edges as the only decoration, a form known on similar pots by Hester Bateman
(1774-89) of London, but the pierced gallery surrounding the top of objects such as coffee pots or urn-shaped
sugar bowls, often in addition to beading, was unmistakably Philadelphian in an age when silver was
becoming more collectable. **47**

For those with a taste for the antique but little
space, bucket forks are among the oldest examples of
American silver, while miniature caudle cups, just over
an inch high, were also very early. Spoons provide the
greatest variety, since in England before 1700 a plethora
of provincial marks, themselves a collector's subject, can
be found on spoons with finely sculptured finials. The
Apostle spoon is a well-known design, with figures on the
end of the usual hexagonal stem and fig-shaped bowl.
In America, the New York hoof or caryatid terminal is
rare, but there is an enormous range of trifids, coffin
end, fiddle and other patterns and in particular of the
picture backs. A Philadelphian 1790 example shows a

38

43 *George III six-piece tea and coffee set, by R & D Hennell, 1797. In the most pleasing neo-classic lines, this set is obviously hand made.*

44 *Two examples of Queen Anne tapersticks, one in the octagonal form, by Matthew Cooper, 1708, the other, one of a pair on circular reeded bases, by John Fawdery, 1705. With them is a heavy George II oval cream-boat on four lion mask and paw supports, by Paul Crespin, 1734.*

45 *George II plain tapering cylindrical coffee pot by Samuel Blackford of Plymouth, circa 1725. All West Country silver was marked in Exeter after 1700 and largely followed London styles.*

dove, wings spread, perched on a tree with a sprig in its beak. The tiny caddy spoons in England cast in endless different shapes, some purely ornamental, are also very popular with collectors. **48** They were well made in Birmingham, which has the anchor as its town mark.

Sugar tongs of the scissor type, with shell grips, were made in America from about 1750, in England somewhat earlier. Their stems were never alike, while later pincher tongs are enormously varied in decoration, and are often bright cut, embossed or pierced and are among the least expensive to buy.

Ingenious and quite delightful are the baby corals and rattles that were made by all nations from the time of the ancient Egyptians to the 19th century. Most of them are beautifully engraved, as are the rows of silver

44

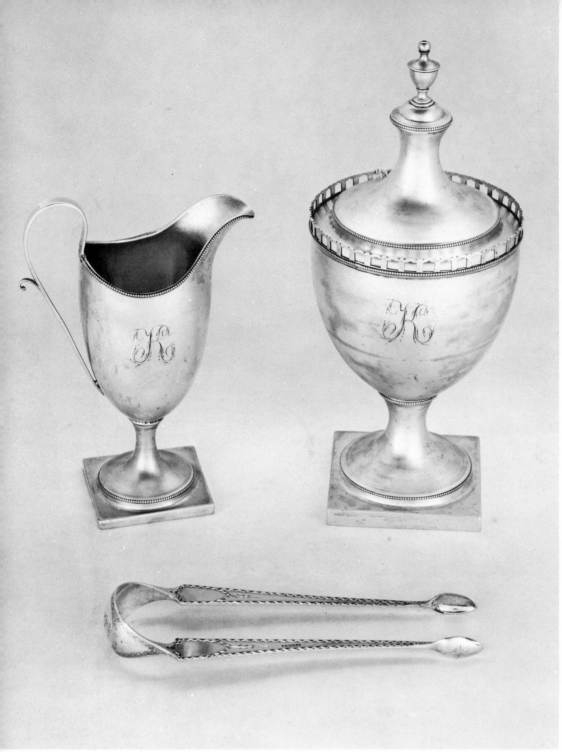

46 *One of a pair of George II soup tureens, covers and stands, complete with liners and matching ladles, by Edward Wakelin, 1755.*

47 *This urn-shaped sugar bowl and cover, with matching creamer and suger tongs, by Robert Swan, Philadelphia, circa 1800, epitomizes all that distinguishes Philadelphian work at the time, with beaded borders and pierced galleries. The initial 'K' leads the enthusiast to discover the family history of General John Kelso.*

bells, and teething whistles. Patch boxes too, were made in most countries, for all ladies like to beautify themselves, and keep their adornments in nicely decorated silver boxes with a detachable lid. Round or oval tobacco boxes were rather larger than patch boxes but had similar lids. Snuff boxes on the other hand had hinged lids since gentlemen took snuff at any time, perhaps on horseback when they would not have both hands free. These were superlatively made in Birmingham as were nutmeg graters, carried individually for the seasoning of food; vinaigrettes, for personal freshness; wine labels and other small objects, all good subjects for collection. Vinaigrettes were especially attractive with their beautifully pierced grilles inside tiny boxes, and were made to look like anything that took the craftsman's fancy, such as a fish, animal, strawberry, or flower basket. **49**

48 *Caddy Spoons. Top row, left to right: a kidney shape, by Cocks and Bettridge, 1813; (b) very rare mussel shell by Francis Higgins, London, 1851; (c) by Josiah Snatt, who made all such hands, London, 1800.*
Bottom row, left to right: Two snuff boxes by Nathaniel Mills, the left showing Newstead Abbey, family home of Lord Byron, sold by him in 1818 to pay his debts; right, Windsor Castle. Between is an unmarked jockey cap spoon, circa 1800.
All filigree caps are unmarked and there is an unproved story that they were made by Italian prisoners-of-war in Clerkenwell

Prison during the Franco-Italian wars. Almost all other jockey caps were made by John Taylor, to whom this is probably ascribed, although Samuel Pemberton also made a few.

49 *Four examples of Birmingham-made boxes, the casket above, by Edward Smith, 1851; the snuff box below it, by Joseph Willmore, 1834, depicting Dryburgh Abbey, and two vinaigrettes, the swans by Gervaise Wheeler, 1838, and York Minster by 'JT', 1834.*

The finest snuff boxes are French, gold and richly jewelled; nevertheless, those made in Birmingham by Nathaniel Mills in the early 19th century are first class, with their repoussé tops, mostly depicting castles, cathedrals and other topographical subjects, and their strongly cast sides or borders. Other makers created boxes with pastoral, sporting, mythological or commemorative scenes, and although snuff boxes were also made in London and elsewhere, on the whole they are less imaginative. The great names of Birmingham displayed the same characteristics in their caddy spoons, vinaigrettes, wine labels and other small things, and between them did more for the small collector than any other group of men.

Short Glossary of Terms.

Acanthus conventional foliage decoration, usually embossed, adopted from the capitals of Corinthian columns and used extensively from the 16th century.

Beading round half circles, like a string of beads, most commonly used as edging decoration in the late 18th century, but also as a 'drop', when the beads diminish in size down the handles of 17th century tankards etc.

Bright cut engraving popular from c 1790; a bevelled cut that removes metal, polishing as it does so.

Caryatid handles thumbpieces cast in form of classic draped females, surmounting handles on some early bowls and cups.

Coffin ended spoons the wide end narrowed by in-sloping cuts, exactly as with a coffin.

Cut card work decoration cut from sheet silver, usually as foliage or strapwork, soldered on to silver as applied decoration in relief after mid 17th century, also serving to strengthen the metal at the joints.

Fiddle pattern violin shouldered stem to a spoon, early 19th century.

Finial the ornament at the tip of a spoon or on a cover, tooled to shape, or more often, cast in a mould.

Flanged lid a flat projection.

Gadrooning a lobed border, giving an indented effect, spiral or straight, of any narrow width.

Meander wire an ornamental wire applied around the moulded base band on early New York tankards, below a rim of stamped ornament.

Patina the outer skin on silver formed through centuries of care.

Strapwork often interlaced ribbons forming panels filled with foliage or scrolls; engraved or flat chased in the 16th century.

Trifid spoons have a flat, three-toed terminal, sometimes with the ends turning upwards. Late 17th century.

CLOCKS AND WATCHES

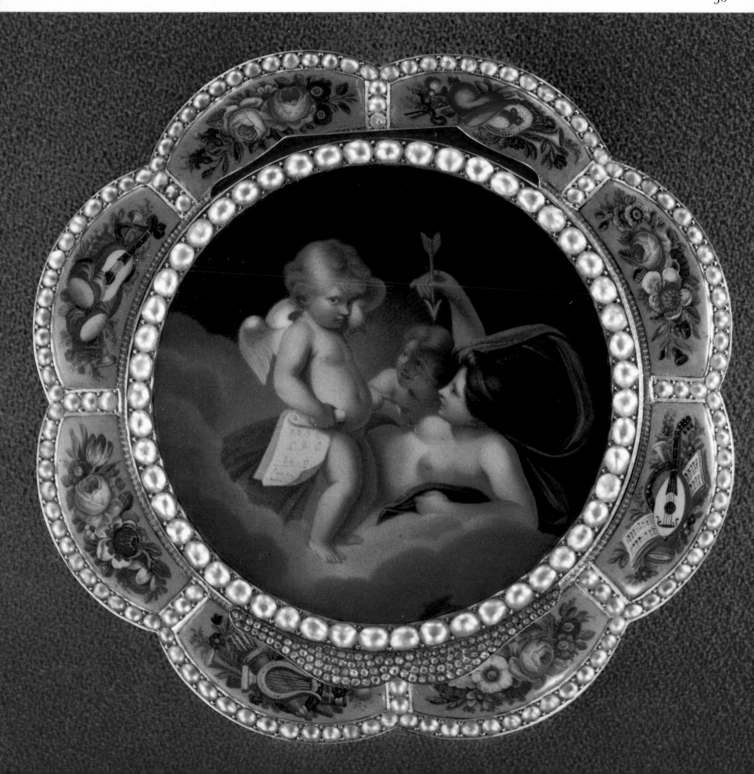

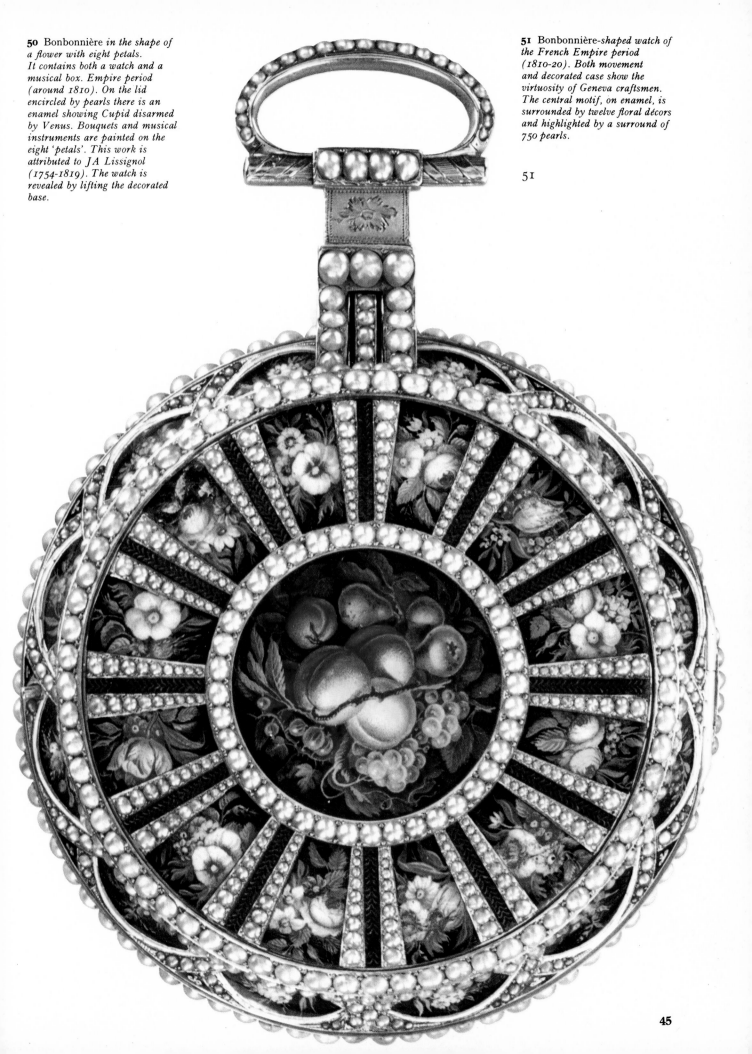

50 Bonbonnière *in the shape of a flower with eight petals. It contains both a watch and a musical box. Empire period (around 1810). On the lid encircled by pearls there is an enamel showing Cupid disarmed by Venus. Bouquets and musical instruments are painted on the eight 'petals'. This work is attributed to J A Lissignol (1754-1819). The watch is revealed by lifting the decorated base.*

51 Bonbonnière-*shaped watch of the French Empire period (1810-20). Both movement and decorated case show the virtuosity of Geneva craftsmen. The central motif, on enamel, is surrounded by twelve floral décors and highlighted by a surround of 750 pearls.*

51

52 *Typical bracket clock from the end of the 17th century. Hour striking with a pull-quarter mechanism. This was made by Thomas Tompion about 1690.*

53 *Detail. The engraved back plate of this Tompion bracket clock gives some idea of the quality of the workmanship for which this maker was famous.*

It is only relatively recently that timekeepers have come to appeal to more than a few dedicated collectors. In the past it was perhaps the complexities hidden within an exquisitely wrought golden case which limited the appeal of old watches, and the problem of keeping a score of 17th and 18th century bracket clocks in going order discouraged people from acquiring them. Things are now greatly changed. There is much more information readily available about escapements, fusees and stackfreeds, strike and repeater mechanisms, calendar and astronomical work to enthuse the would-be collector, and this has had its effect. More and more people are now collecting in this field, a fact which is vouched for by the all too familiar pattern of escalating prices.

Movements, however, which have come to be recognized as being at least as important as the cases that contain them, can be one of the main drawbacks to collecting timekeepers. A clock or a watch is not really a clock or watch at all unless it is capable of ticking. Getting a mechanism that is 200 years old to go and to keep it in going condition, can be an expensive business, always supposing one can find someone to do the work. There are today few craftsmen capable of replacing missing or broken parts and refurbishing worn ones. In the future, there are likely to be fewer still. As the value of an old clock or watch either as a possession, or at auction, is very closely related to its ability to function, and to the authenticity of its movement, this is a disturbing situation for existing collectors. It is also a factor which anyone who is considering coming into the collecting field would be well advised to bear in mind.

There are a number of collectors who, foreseeing this development, have turned themselves into horolo-

gical hobbyists. Having diligently acquired the skills of a repairer, they now spend a great deal of their time bent over their workbenches restoring and servicing their possessions. They find that this is not only a useful accomplishment, but it has greatly increased their understanding and appreciation of the craftsmen of the past.

Anyone coming new to any field of collecting will find it difficult to know where to begin. Either he can set about assembling an historical record of the craft, acquiring representative pieces from every period, or he can specialize. The tendency today seems to be to do the latter. But in what to specialize? The answer to this question depends mainly on financial resources, on availability, and, of course, on personal taste.

Obviously, anyone who wants to collect the works of that great master of English clock and watch making, Thomas Tompion, will have to be very wealthy. **52** Tompion worked at the period of the great timekeeping revolution at the beginning of the second half of the 17th century, which followed the invention of the balance-spring and the first application of a pendulum to a clock. He was the most accomplished of a small band of watch and clock makers whose contribution to the revolution was to raise standards of craftsmanship. They cut their wheels and pinions with a new accuracy and produced their escapements to ever closer tolerances. Their productions were elegant as well as accurate. These makers brought in accomplished engravers to ornament the brass plates that supported their trains, and took full advantage of the skills of the jewellers and the cabinet makers of the time to encase their movements in precious metals and woods. **53**

Today a Tompion clock can fetch anything from £5,800 ($15,000) to £23,000 ($60,000) or more, but no collector who could afford one would feel he is being overcharged. A Tompion watch in a gold case could be bought much more cheaply. A good one might fetch £385 ($1,000) or more at auction.

Another hunting ground for the wealthy collector is the watches of Breguet, which command much higher prices even than those of Tompion. **65** Abraham Louis Breguet was a Swiss working in Paris in the Napoleonic era, and his work appeals particularly to those whose chief interest lies in mechanisms. He was beyond question the greatest watchmaker who ever polished a pinion. The watches that came out of his workshops are as beautifully made as they are ingenious, and if his cases and dials are seldom decorative they are in perfect taste and beautifully proportioned. As a final example of the riches

which a clock and watch collector could aspire to, there are the French clocks made during the reigns of Louis XV and Louis XVI. These are quite superb essays in ornamentation. **57**

To specialize in collecting watches rather than clocks has much to recommend it. There is still less competition in this field, and therefore, if price is an important consideration, there will not be the same limitation on what can be bought. More important for many people today is the fact that watches take up little room.

Outside museums, the drum-shaped or spherical watches of the 16th century are few and far between. But there are a good many 17th century watches about, even a fair number of the charming form watches made early in the century. These little toys in the form of crosses, stars, shells and skulls usually have cases made of brass, ornamented by engraving or chasing, and sometimes with inserts of rock crystal. **59** A single hand traversed the chapter ring, indication enough of the shortcoming of these watches as timekeepers. Their charm is their chief attraction, which is why they can be picked up for as little as £ 58 ($ 150).

These watches were superseded quite early in the century by larger but not much more accurate watches, very like modern pocket watches. Their cases were decorated with enamel. At first the designs used were typical 17th century floral arabesques, like those found on miniature cases of the period, which were proliferated by the pattern books of the time. Then came the superb painted enamels from Blois and Geneva, usually depicting classical and biblical scenes.

At the end of the 17th century the famous pair-cases made their appearance. These were the cases brought in by Tompion, Quare and their contemporaries to house their movements. The inner of these two cases was usually a decorative gold one. At the end of the century it was often chased repoussé with heroic scenes. The outer case was sometimes of gold too, but often of studded leather or shagreen. The watches of this period, fitted with the new hair-spring, offered their owners fairly accurate timekeeping for their money, and sometimes, remarkably after all these years, watches from this period can still be found which are capable of keeping time within a few minutes a week.

In the 18th century the case was modified by fashion. Baroque repoussé gave place to the rococo. In England the gold dial was replaced by the enamel one

already popular in France. Then came a period of classical plainness, followed by a new age of ebullience towards the end of the century when circlets of half pearls were placed around the dial and case decoration became again the prerogative of the enamellers. During this century matching chatelaines added distinction to some of the watches, but rather unexpectedly usually add little to the price a collector has to pay today.

These shifts of fashion, and the variety of the examples to survive, make the 18th century a happy hunting ground for the collector. The clocks and watches of this age are also particularly interesting to the collector with a mechanical bent. He can always be on the lookout for early examples of the jewelling invented by Facio and the Debaufré brothers in 1704, of the shock protection first incorporated in a watch towards the end of the century by Breguet, or for evidence of the ceaseless search for accuracy in the form of new escapements and variations on already established ones. Then there are those early experiments in self-winding, employing the pedometer principle to be looked for in watches made by Perrelet, Recordon and Breguet.

The craftsmanship of the 19th century has increasingly attracted collectors as earlier work has become scarcer and more expensive. This has resulted in a greater understanding of this period, and what once was generally despised now turns out to have charms of its own. The return to the idea of a watch as a toy rather than as a serious instrument for measuring the passing of time led to the production of fanciful form watches in the early years of the century. Watches were tucked into the bases of tiny enamelled harps and mandolines, hidden in flower baskets, secreted in miniature violins and in toy dogs and such whimsies appealed enormously to the woman of the day. Enamelled gold watches continued to be made as well as the fanciful novelties, **50**, **51**, and it was not until well into the 20th century that the Geneva enamellers finally ceased to enrich watches with subtle colours, produced by compounding powdered glass and metallic oxides.

There have always been those who found clocks more fascinating than watches. Clocks have a longer history than watches, and it is possible for a collector to aspire to specimens as early as the 15th century. Iron wall clocks of the 15th and 16th centuries, while not to be found every day, do come on the market from time to time, and 16th century spring powered drum clocks, with horizontal dials, are also still collectable items.

54

The first distinctive English clock was the brass lantern of the 17th century, so called because its square form, with pillars at the corners under an arched top, was a popular one for lanterns at this time. **60** These clocks, which were weight driven and needed winding every thirty hours, were made over a long period, the earliest before 1620 and the last ones well into the 18th century. Lantern clocks should not be bought carelessly. There are probably more fakes and reproductions on the market than there are genuine ones, and even those which are partly genuine have often been so altered and botched over the centuries as to lose much of their value and interest. A lantern clock with two hands should always arouse suspicion. It could be genuine, but it almost certainly will prove to be a fake.

The golden age of English clockmaking, the last forty years of the 17th century, produced the most collectable of all clocks. First came those early, elegant, long cased clocks produced by the Fromanteel family, with pillared and porticoed hoods and narrow trunks designed to hold the weights that provided the power for the verge movements and the striking trains.

Then came the bigger, long cased clocks made following the invention of the much superior anchor escapement by John Clement in the 1670s. With this escapement the Royal Pendulum, some thirty-nine inches long and with a swing of four or five degrees was used. To accommodate this a wider trunk was needed, and this is a feature of long clock cases made after 1685. The best of these long clock cases were superb pieces of cabinet making, richly veneered or decorated with the intricacies of marquetry work. From the outset these

54 *French ormolu clock with Sèvres china shaped panels painted with Watteau figures and with four boy mounts.*

55 *Fine example of the work of the 19th century English clockmaker Benjamin Lewis Vulliamy.*

56 *Important James Cox architectural clock in agate with chased and repoussé gilt-metal mounts, signed and dated 1766. Below: a separate watch mechanism gives the phases of the moon one side and minutes on the reverse, this movement operating the carillon which plays four melodies.*

56

55

clocks were very accurate by the standards of the day. Following the work done on the temperature compensation of pendulums by Graham and the Harrisons in the early 18th century this accuracy was even further improved.

Side by side with the development of the long case, the bracket clock evolved. **58** This had a spring powered movement usually fitted with a pyramidical fusee to compensate for the decreasing force of the drive as the clock ran down. Knibb, Windmills, Quare and Graham as well as Tompion made outstanding examples, which usually had ebonized cases, and tended to be increasingly enriched with gilt-brass mounts as the years passed.

It was unusual for a family to own more than one bracket clock, and a carrying handle to allow it to be transported from room to room was an invariable fea-

ture. Sometimes too bracket clocks were provided with a travelling box.

Changes in the style of cases and dials allow us to recognize the bracket clocks and long cases of the 18th century from those of the 17th. The long cases spouted finials in the form of urns and balls, and developed broken arches. The bracket clocks were given enamel dials, and the cases lost some of their solidity. Similar divergencies of style made it easy to recognize Continental clocks from English ones, even before the ebullience of the Louis XV style set first the French, and later most Continental clocks, apart from the more sober English ones. **54** English clocks made in the second half of the 18th century can be bought for as little as £ 77 ($ 200), so that this is a good area for the collector of limited means.

57 *The combination of the work of one of the great Paris clockmakers, Estienne Le Noir, and the rare Chantilly porcelain account for the fact that this Louis XV ormolu clock made in 1740 sold for £31,650 ($82,320) in Christie's in 1966.*

58 *A rare example of a late 17th century bracket clock by Henry Jones. The movement has verge escapement, outside locking plate and Dutch striking, and the dial is decorated with cherub spandrels and a calender aperture with the signature 'Henry Jones in Ye Temple' engraved at the base. The case is of oak veneered with burr walnut, circa 1685.*

Clocks made in America during the 18th century were European in style, and were made mostly by craftsmen who had served their apprenticeship in England, Holland or Germany. Thus the clocks they made were either British inspired long cases with horned tops, or the *wag-on-wall*, with unenclosed weights and pendulum, similar to the wall clocks popular over a long period in Holland and Germany. The work of makers such as David Rittenhouse, Benjamin Franklin, Thomas Harland, Thomas Claggett and Daniel Burnap is greatly sought after by collectors today.

It was an apprentice of Daniel Burnap, Eli Terry, who revolutionized American clockmaking. The Willards, of Massachusetts, are said to have invented the shelf-clock, the first distinctive American type, by condensing the long case. It was Terry, however, who gave the new clock its own style and who produced it in quan-

tity. His pillar and scroll shelf clocks were so called because he placed slender pillars on either side of the oblong cases, usually topped off with urn finials, and he also decorated the tops and bottoms of his cases with scrollwork. Below the dials of gaily painted iron there was a glass panel painted all over with floral motifs or a naïve landscape, except for a circular area in the centre through which the owner could watch the wagging pendulum.

Originally, the movements, like those of many of the earlier American long cases, were made of wood. Only later was brass available in sufficient quantity to allow Terry to produce metal movements for the great quantity of clocks he turned out from his factory.

The pillar and scroll clocks were also produced in the factories of Seth Thomas and Silas Hoadley who

had collaborated with Terry in the early days, and in a host of small workshops. They remained in fashion until an apprentice of Terry's produced a new type of shelf clock in 1825 to challenge their hold on the market.

Chauncey Jerome mass-produced tens of thousands of his bronze and looking-glass shelf clocks, undercutting all the other makers by selling them for upwards of 75 cents (30 p) each. With brass mounts and looking glass doors, these clocks were made in a variety of shapes, and were exported to Europe in considerable numbers in the 1840s before Chauncey Jerome's spectacular bankruptcy.

In 1802, Simon Willard patented what has been called 'America's most important artistic contribution in horology', the banjo clock. This was usually fitted with high quality movements, consisting of a dial in a

61 *Left to right: French strike-repeating carriage clock by Soldano with four porcelain panels contained in a bamboo-style case; rare English carriage timepiece with a compass on the top and thermometers at either side of the case. The gilt brass is finely engraved and four dolphins set off the compass on the top; French strike-repeating carriage clock contained in serpentine-shaped gilt brass case with three ivory panels hand painted with 18th century scenes.*

circular surround surmounted with an elaborate finial. Below this was a narrow trunk to which was attached a square box in which the pendulum swung, visible through a circle of glass, inset into the veneered front. Later these clocks were varied in design. The lyre clock which derived from French models had a gracefully curving lyre-shaped body below the dial surround instead of an angular one. They usually stood on a matching bracket instead of being attached to the wall. Another variation on the banjo was the so-called girandole which had a circular instead of a square base. This is today the most sought after of all American antique clocks.

Unlike clocks, American watches are not very rewarding to collect. Of the few watches made in America 63 before 1850, the great majority were based on European movements, and those that were not have little to recommend them. It was only in the second half of the 19th century that America made a valuable contribution to the history of watchmaking, when the names Ingersol and Waterbury became world famous, and the mass-produced American watch could be sold at a price that made it available to millions all over the world.

Two types of clocks produced in Europe in the 19th century are particularly interesting to collectors. The simple and charming little French carriage clocks, with their glass panelled brass cases, giving glimpses of the movement within, appeal to many people and are varied enough in detail to absorb the collector. **61** Then there are those incredible *tours-de-force*, that were first produced in France in the 1780s and continued to be made throughout the 19th century all over Europe. These ranged in complexity from the restrained neo-classicism of the Vulliamy clocks to those Eastern nightmares which James Cox created for the Chinese market. **55, 56** It is difficult to believe that the Chinese could really have liked this piling of camels on elephants and dragons, building up to a tiny and undistinguished enamel clock dial, looking completely out of place on top of it all. But they are great fun, as are so many of the clocks which reveal the penchant of the 19th century for romantic dreams of distant times and places. Late examples in this vein can still be picked up in bric-à-brac shops for a small sum.

Space does not allow for more than a few of the types of clocks and watches of the past to be mentioned here. I would have liked to mention the night clocks, the rolling ball clocks, the wooden clocks made in the Black Forest and in America, and the decorative wall-clocks from Friesland, which are rising dramatically in price as more collectors succumb to their fascinations.

62 *Two French watches, circa 1700 and mid-17th century; and a mid-17th century german alarm watch.*

64 *French Carriage clock with calendar dials and leather protective case.*

63 *Form watch in the shape of a cross with hinged rock crystal cover made in the late 16th century, probably in Germany.*

65 *An outstanding example of the work of Abraham-Louis Breguet. The gold dial at the front shows the time. The rear calendar dial is of platinum. It cost its first owner General Junot, 5,160 francs in 1807. It sold at Sotheby's in 1964 for £27,500 ($71,500).*

64

65

66 A fine topaz and silver mounted sevigne, Spanish, circa 1760.

67 A collection of coloured stone jewelry showing some of the many styles current from about 1840 to 1890. The earliest show a delicate scrolling appearance, though early in the Queen's reign large cabochon garnets were fashionable for the double and treble pendant brooches worn. Snakes remained a favourite theme, while travel abroad brought a vogue for Italian mosaic jewelry. The Etruscan style with its granulated patterns came in about 1860 and survived for some twenty years, while about the same time came the technique of mounting gems and gold on other stones or enamels. The small fringed pendant bears a registration mark for 1872. The larger fringed brooch shows the style of the aesthetic movement.

59

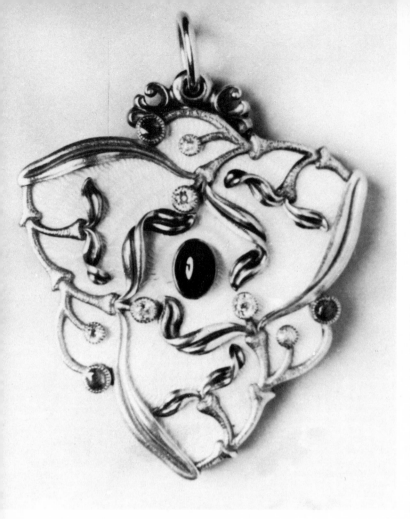

68 *Enamel and gem stone mirror locket of gold, late 19th century by Fabergé (Russian).*

69 *Swallows by Lalique, enamel on gold. The feeling of movement and action in jewelry was a contribution of this Art Nouveau period.*

jewelry took forms similar to modern jewelry, such as necklaces, rings, bracelets, brooches, pins and beads. Only diadems were singular to that period. Often they were placed on victors' heads at athletic events.

Renaissance Jewelry

The first noteworthy period for jewelry was the Renaissance. The magnificent pieces created at that time were comparatively few in number and extremely expensive. **71** They were made primarily for Royalty or for dignitaries of the Church. The middle class citizen did not use jewelry until the end of the 18th century. The finer pieces of Renaissance jewelry are now prohibitively expensive. There are still some lesser pieces available at modest cost which are of great interest to collectors.

Hat ornaments called *enseignes* were very popular at this time. The fashion for cameo portraits was especially appealing to Royalty who had their pictures painted and set into jeweled frames by goldsmiths. Famous painters and architects created designs for jewelry with great pride. In the 16th century the robes worn by Royalty were studded with pearls and jewels. Enamelling achieved a high refinement, and the setting of a piece of jewelry assumed far more importance than the stones. Artistry in cutting stones had not yet developed and the backs of gems were still covered with gold or silver from the setting, but the reverse side of gold jeweled pieces was finished in a fine manner.

18th Century Jewelry

After the development of the brilliant cut, in about 1700, greater emphasis was placed on the gem stone rather than design and enamel work. Attention was given to bringing out the brilliance of gems, and most of them were set with silver rather than with gold. About this time the middle classes began to buy jewelry. Large pieces were being worn, especially with the diamonds set in silver *en tremblant* which moved with body movement. The gems sparkled in candlelight and attracted attention by their size and brilliance. The back of the gem setting now also opened to allow the light to shine through and enhance the stones. In Hungary, during the same period, enamelling still predominated and there was great emphasis on copying Renaissance pieces. Many of these Hungarian pieces are available and are valued as collectors' items.

19th Century Jewelry

Perhaps the greatest era of jewelry making was that of the 19th century, particularly in France and Eng-

For thousands of years jewelry has been one of man's most prized possessions. Whether worn as a charm to protect against disease or danger, tucked away as an investment, purchased at great price to adorn milady's person, or in the market place of the poor for one's beloved, jewelry has become highly desired. Passed from generation to generation, it is loved and treasured in most intimate ways. It has sometimes driven man to commit crimes, but it has also brought joy and security beyond description.

What is in jewelry that has endowed it with such power? There is certainly something more than its intrinsic value, for many pieces of old and once highly valued jewelry have little material worth when broken down. What then is its power? Undoubtedly, it is in the eye of the beholder – a thing of beauty and joy, of love and attachment.

Classic Jewelry

During Greek, Roman and Etruscan periods, jewelry was treasured principally for its gold. The workmanship was not especially sophisticated, the design was simple and appealing, but hardly the work of genius. Precious stones were rare or unknown at the time. Most of the important gold pieces of jewelry are on exhibit in museums, and authentic pieces of importance are not too common in antique shops, though a few fine pieces occasionally come up for auction. Except for the cameos, most of the classic jewelry has little appeal for modern women. Even the elaborately granulated Etruscan pieces are roughly finished, and scarcely compare, for adornment, with similar jewelry produced by Castellani and other British goldsmiths in the 19th century. Classic

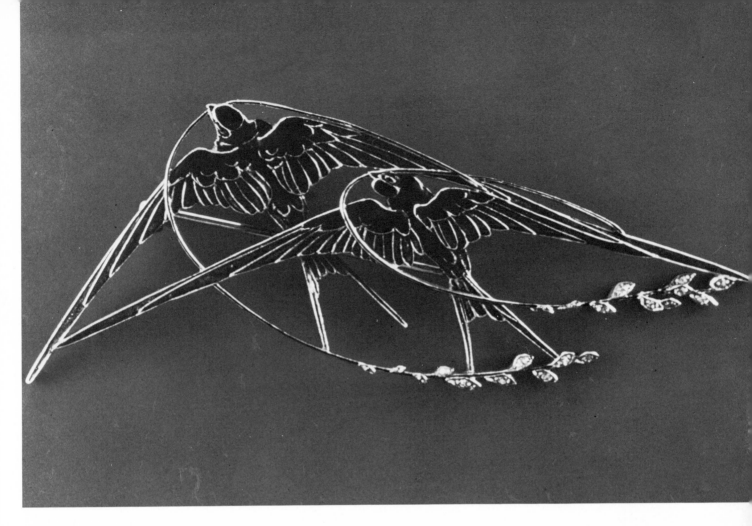

land. But America also began to establish fine concerns around that time. While there were still many excellent goldsmiths in these countries who handmade outstanding pieces of jewelry, machine made pieces supplied the needs of the overwhelming demand for the average citizen.

Collecting Antique Jewelry

Antique jewelry can be exciting, since not only is it beautiful and interesting, but it can be worn and admired every day and enjoyed as a conversation piece. It can also be a good investment if chosen wisely. Unlike the modern type sold in most shops, good antique pieces do not depreciate shortly after purchase; rather they appreciate with time.

Most collectors agree that it is better to buy one good piece with whatever money one is able to spend than many small and inferior pieces that are less desirable. This applies whether one is buying a single piece to wear, or a specialized collector's piece. Most collectors buy antique jewelry to wear, while dealers buy to sell. Interestingly enough, the most serious and sophisticated collectors and connoisseurs of antique jewelry have been, and still are, men. They try to buy exceptional pieces for their inherent workmanship and artistic interest. These pieces are generally the kind seen as exhibits in museums.

Among the most eminent collectors in history are Medici (Italy), Gulbenkian (Portugal), Esmerian (New York), Gutman (New York) and Citroen (Holland). Most collectors of fine jewelry, however, prefer to remain anonymous.

Such a variety of jewelry was produced in the 19th century that the fields open to both the wealthy and less well off collectors are endless. For most of us with limited means, opportunities for collecting fall especially in the following categories: shell and stone cameos, jet, memorial and hair jewelry, mosaic pieces, silver, steel, iron and paste jewelry, many of which have been unappreciated. **69** American Indian, Mexican, turquoise, and coral jewelry is still plentiful and inexpensive.

Many collectors are interested in functional pieces such as stick pins, bracelets, hair combs, earrings, shoe buckles, rings, scarf pins and charms. Some collectors seek jewelry depicting animals and insects, such as dogs, butterflies, moths, dragonflies, beetles, and even gargoyle-like figures. One of the most beautiful collections I have ever seen consisted of enamel dragonflies and butterflies with moveable wings and inexpensive gem stones. I have also seen jewelry collections of lizards and monkeys, elephants and donkeys, seals, and pencils that elongate by twisting a top crested with coloured stone.

One might even be interested in collecting English jewelry with an Egyptian motif, introduced by important archaeological discoveries in the 19th century; or with an East India look, made popular when India affiliated with the Commonwealth.

Collecting enamel jewelry is another exciting speciality, for countless pieces are available that are inexpensive but reflect much artistic design and craftsmanship. Collecting handmade enamel jewelry is an important speciality because of its beauty and delicate workmanship, especially if the enamelling is translucent. In England a special type called *Jubilee Enamel* was created to celebrate Victoria's 50th anniversary as Queen. The colouring is gay and glistening.

70

71

70 *Tiara enamelled on both sides with gem stones in a gothic style. English, probably by Wilson or Murphy, 1910.*

71 *Renaissance eagle with stones and enamel. This was purchased during the past five years for less than £200 ($480).*

72 *Enamel and gem studded watch in revival of Renaissance style. Boucheron, French about 1800.*

73 *Chatelaine watch with intricate gold work and cabochon sapphires. Marcus and Co, USA, early 1900s.*

74 *Delicate cameo of stone set in pearl and diamond frame. English mid-19th century.*

72

73

75

Another neglected field is that created by the Arts and Crafts Movement in England towards the end of the 19th century. Available in silver and gold, these distinctive pieces are of historical value, a value which should increase in the future. Small pieces of Art Nouveau are quite available and inexpensive. **78**

If one has the means one might be able to collect the fabulous gold and enamel works of Giuliano or the finely granulated jewelry of Castellani, both Italians who worked in England during the 19th century. **75** In the United States a few farsighted collectors are seeking jewelry made by outstanding firms such as Tiffany, Marcus and Company, Caldwell, and Jenson.

How to Select Authentic Antique Jewelry

Most important in selecting good antique jewelry is the assessing of workmanship. Inexpensive pieces are reproduced but not to simulate original pieces, because it is unprofitable, and it is not difficult to distinguish between a recent reproduction and a piece of jewelry made in the Victorian period. Generally, the reproduction appears new and unused. It shows the regular and finished edges that result from being stamped and put together by machines, and it shows also a high degree of finish. Stones are in an obviously machine made setting which is very regular around the edges. Inexpensive reproductions are not signed. If made of gold, a 14 carat mark is stamped on them, and they are quite likely to bear an American maker's mark.

It is always proper to ask the salesman or jeweler from whom one purchases a piece of jewelry whether it is new or antique. Then one can return it if it is found to be a reproduction, bearing in mind that good pieces of anti-

que jewelry appreciate while new pieces generally do not appreciate for many years. Important pieces of jewelry of all periods and styles are often reproduced and even signed with counterfeit signatures in order to command higher prices. Many dealers themselves are not certain about authenticity. Be careful, therefore, that excellent workmanship is present in an expensive piece of jewelry. Most good pieces are finished almost as well on the reverse side as they are on the front.

Prior to about 1850, comparatively few pieces of jewelry were signed, even if they were important pieces. It was only in the late 19th century, and especially by Art Nouveau goldsmiths, that jewelry was signed. In some pieces the signature was on the pin which may have broken and been removed. Or when a brooch, for instance, was made into a pendant, the signature could inadvertently have been removed. In jewelry made by goldsmiths such as Lalique, every fine piece was personally stamped with the goldsmith's name or maker's mark. **69** Fine English goldsmiths such as Giuliano, Castellani, Brogdan, and Hancock, also signed most of their important pieces. Other goldsmiths, however, rarely signed their jewelry and purchasers have to be familiar with the characteristics of jewelry made by Ashby and Wilson or Murphy, since they did not sign all their work.

In the United States, Marcus and Company, Baily, Banks and Biddle, Caldwell and Tiffany signed most of their important pieces and their signatures add prestige and assurance of fine workmanship.

For many centuries France was the leader in designing and producing excellent jewelry. In the 19th century outstanding jewelers in this country were

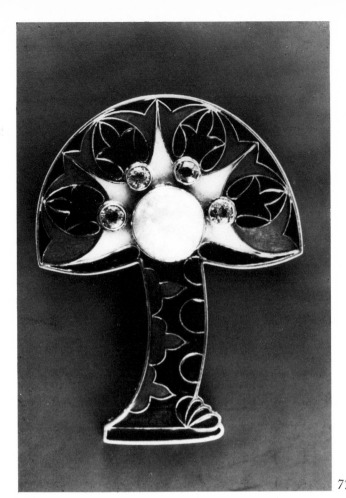

77

78

F. Meurice, Bapst, Fontenay, Wiese, Falize and Boucheron. **72** Every country, however, made its distinctive contribution and style to jewelry. There is no mistaking, for example, a piece of jewelry made in Hungary, and the meticulous craftsmanship of Russian goldsmiths such as Fabergé is very characteristic. **68**

Giuliano and Castellani's work was also distinctive, the latter having carefully developed the Etruscan method of granulation to the point of being meticulous and finished. In the United States Tiffany and Marcus companies also developed their own styles as did Cartier and Van Cleaf and Arpels. **73** Probably the most distinctive style in England was created by the Arts and Crafts Movement.

Several marks may be stamped or engraved on gold French Art Nouveau jewelry. The minimum gold standard for French jewelry in the 1900s was 18 carat (750 thousandths). In January 1864 the mark ET was created to be stamped on gold plate that met the French standard and came from countries without customs conventions. In June 1893 this mark was replaced by an owl in an oval frame for gold plate coming into France.

Neither the ET mark nor the owl emblem necessarily dates a piece, rather does it show the time when it was brought into France and assayed. Pieces of Art Nouveau gold jewelry made in Paris should be stamped with an eagle's head to designate compliance with the gold standard. If a piece of jewelry in the Art Nouveau style is made of gold, of less than 18 carat, it is not likely to be French. In America, 14 carat was used most commonly, and in England and the rest of Europe the gold was between 9 and 18 carat.

75 *Enamel pearl and diamond brooch by Giuliano. English, mid-19th century.*

76 *Translucent enamel brooch in gold. Masriera, Portugal, about 1900.*

77 *Mushroom brooch with enamel on both sides, on gold base, and with a large fire opal. Signed by HG Murphy. English, circa 1910.*

78 *Large beehive brooch with fresh water pearls and enamels, by Paul Lienard. French, about 1900.*

65

CERAMICS
A General Introduction

From the primitive earthenware of ancient times to the sophisticated products of the 18th century that have been produced the world over, there is a wealth from which to choose, if the collector brings his own knowledge, taste and enthusiasm to bear on the problems of discovery and attribution.

A basic knowledge at least of the various aspects of the potter's craft, and the terms used to describe them, is not merely desirable but essential for anyone hoping to build up a collection. He will learn as he goes along, getting to know the physical feel of the things, their texture and weight as well as their outward appearance.

First, there is the distinction between two allied materials. The word *pottery* is used, in a general sort of way, to cover just about everything made by a potter, but in a special sense it describes various kinds of earthenware and *stoneware*, as distinct from *porcelain* or *china*.

Pottery is the name for anything made of common clay – earthenware – and which is allowed to dry in the heat of the sun or baked – *fired* – in a kiln. It is usually porous unless glazed, and is opaque, so that not even a strong light can pass through it.

Stoneware is very hard pottery, which is fired at a high temperature and often 'salt-glazed' when salt is thrown into the kiln. However, at its best it is so hard and close-grained that it requires no glaze to be watertight, and can even be cut on a wheel like flint glass. It is usually opaque, but can be sometimes semi-translucent.

Porcelain (hard-paste) is the 'true' porcelain, which was made first in China and later in Europe by mixing china clay (kaolin) with rotten china rock *(petuntse)* and firing it at a very high temperature (about 1,350°C). It is very hard in texture and, usually, in appearance. It is translucent except when used in a solid mass, as for figures.

Porcelain (soft-paste) is '*false*' porcelain made by adding materials *other* than china rock to china clay; for example in England bone-ash and soap-rock were added, while glassy substances were used on the Continent. It was fired at lower temperatures than *hard-paste*, and is translucent to very varying degrees.

Bone China is an English modification of *hard-paste* made by the addition of bone-ash to the formula, and has been in general use in Britain since the early 19th century. It is stable and consistently translucent.

Glaze is a glassy coating applied to the surface of a pot by dipping or brushing on and it can be either clear or coloured. In the Far East, the glaze was usually applied to the pot after it had dried naturally *(leather-dry)* but *before* the first firing. In the West, it was applied *after* the first or *biscuit* firing. Unglazed porcelain is thus known as *biscuit* or *bisque*, and when enamel colours are painted directly on to the unglazed body the process is termed 'enamelling on the biscuit'.

Under-glaze and *over-glaze*. If the pot is to be glazed, the range of colours that can be applied *before* glazing is limited to those which will withstand the temperature necessary to vitrify the glaze. Painting in these colours, of which the commonest is cobalt blue, is called *under-glaze decoration*. A far wider range of enamel colours, and gilding, can be applied over the glaze, after the first firing, and are then burnt in at a relatively low temperature that does not harm them.

Marks. Many collectors are obsessed with marks, but though of great interest and usefulness, they are not always reliable evidence as the pirating and forging of them has been only too prevalent a practice for centuries past. Until well into the 19th century, only a few European factories were at all consistent with their systems of marking, and a great many first-class pieces have no marks whatsoever. The marks illustrated are only a very small sample of the thousands recorded.

Marks on Pottery and Porcelain

There are over 5,000 marks recorded, and so this minute selection has been made to show, as a warning against the dangers of jumping to conclusions, the visual similarity existing between many belonging to different factories and different periods.

1 *Nast, rue Popincourt, Paris. Mid-19th century.*

2 *Sèvres, period of Second Empire, 1854-70. Numeral indicates year.*

3 *Naples, second period, from about 1760.**

4 *Worcester, 1755-75, imitating Chinese seal mark.**

5 *Chinese seal mark, reign of Yung Chêng, 1723-36.*

6 *Japanese 'felicitation' mark meaning 'happiness' on some Kaga Kutani.*

7 *Rouen, late-17th – early-18th centuries.*

8 *Capodimonte, from 1736, and Buen Retiro, from about 1760.*

9 *Vincennes, 1738-56, then Sèvres. Interlaced 'L's standard, fleur-de-lis only occasionally present.**

10 *Meissen (star period, 1774-1815). Crossed swords standard mark until modern times.**

11 *Bristol (champion's factory, 1770-81) imitating Meissen.*

12 *Pottschappell, near Bonn, 19th-20th centuries.*

13 *Venice, Cozzi factory, 1765-1812.*

14 *Chelsea 'red-anchor', 1752-6.**

15 *Chelsea 'gold-anchor', 1756-69.**

16 *Chelsea-Derby, in gold, 1769-84.*

17 *Bow – on figures, 1760-76.*

18 *Davenport, 1793-1820.*

19 *Derby, 1782-1800. (Early marks in puce, later in red.)*

20 *Derby, Stevenson & Hancock, 1861-1935.*

21 *Worcester, Barr, Flight & Barr, 1807-13.*

22 *Ludwigsburg, 1758-1806.*

23 *Niderviller, from 1792. (Compare coronet with crown, No. 22.)*

24 *Sèvres, 1829-30. (Numeral indicates date on 19th-century wares.)*

25 *Höchst, 18th century.*

26 *Höchst, 19th century.*

27 *St Cloud, early-18th century.**

28 *Doccia, from 1735.*

29 *Worcester, Kerr & Binns, 1852-62.*

30 *Worcester, 1862 onwards.*

31 *Dutch Delft. Albrecht de Keizer, from 1642.**

32 *Dutch Delft. Antoni Kruisweg, from 1740.**

33 *Meissen. Monogram of Augustus Rex, from about 1725 – much imitated by Wolfsohn, Dresden, in 19th century.**

34 *Meissen, 'King's Porcelain Manufactory', from about 1725.*

35 *Berlin, 1837-44. The sceptre, with subtle variations, occurs alone during most periods.*

36 *Scheibe, 19th-20th centuries.*

* These are the marks most flagrantly forged.

N...
a
Paris

1

S N 54

2

3

4

5

6

C

7

8

9

10

3

11

T

12

13

14

15

16

17

DAVENPORT

18

19

S H
D

20

BFB

21

22

23

DÉCORÉ
À SÈVRES
62 29

24

25

D

26

27

28

51

29

51

30

AK

31

AK

32

A

33

K.P.M.

34

K.P.M

35

K.P.M

36

POTTERY

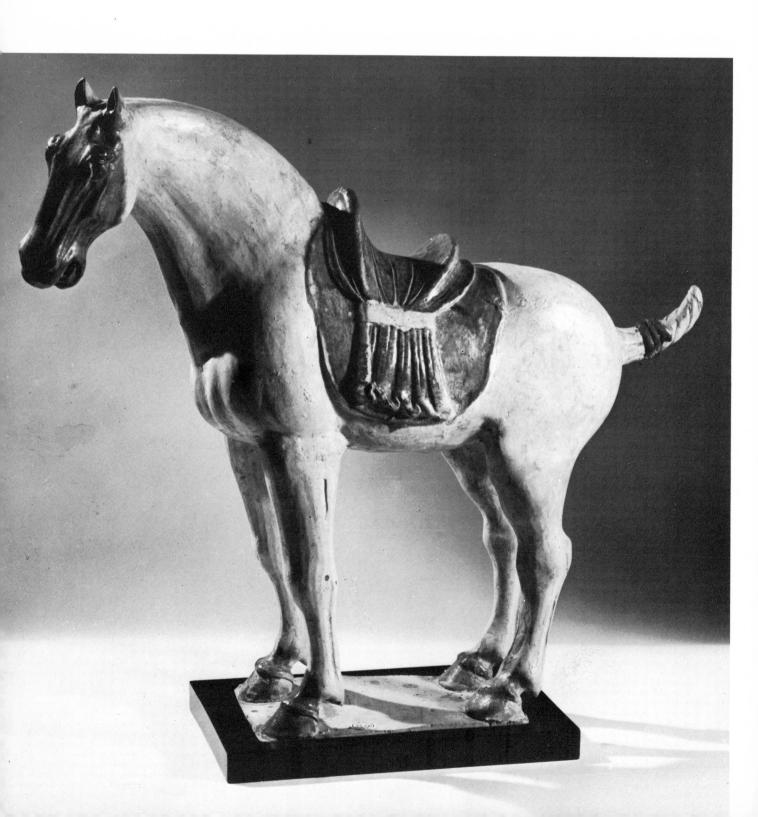

79 *Chinese pottery model of a standing horse, covered in a fine cream and brown glaze. T'ang Dynasty.*

80 *Greek black-figure vase circa 500 BC.*

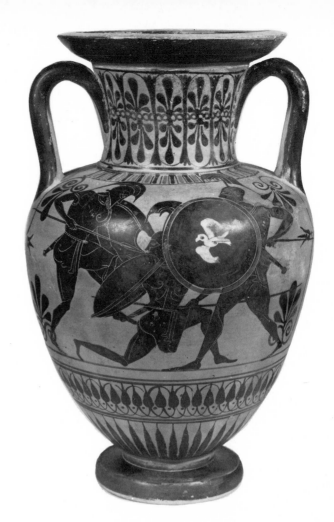

The foregoing remarks may be found of some help in understanding the language spoken by enthusiasts for ceramics in general, and what follows is a slightly more detailed account of the main classes of pottery, as distinct from porcelain. It is not easy to separate them in discussion, so closely do they resemble each other at certain times and in certain places. Often they were in fierce competition with each other; many factories (for example Spode and Swansea) made both simultaneously; and some claimed to have made porcelain when, in fact, the product was a variety of stoneware. It is, however, customary to deal with pottery and porcelain under separate headings, if only because there is a marked, though not always understandable, tendency on the part of collectors to concentrate on one or the other.

Chinese funerary figures

As the Chinese invented porcelain at an early date, and their products thereafter are considered under that heading, the chief interest in their earthenware is centred on the pots and figures buried in tombs during the Han and T'ang dynasties – roughly 200 BC – 900 AD. Originally these clay figures of animals and humans were intended to take the place in the grave of the living horses, servants, wives and dancing girls belonging to a man of importance, all of whom had, in earlier times, been buried with him when he died. To this humanitarian concession we owe the splendid T'ang horses, with or without riders, made of a reddish-brown clay which may be glazed or may show only traces of pigment. **79** Funerary pieces apart, the T'ang potters made some splendid pots with dappled green and yellow glazes.

Greek and Roman

The pottery of Ancient Greece and Rome is normally thought of as something quite apart – 'antiquities' rather than 'antiques', but it is as well for the collector of things nearer our own day to take note, at least, of their existence. They survive in sufficient quantity for the private buyer to be able to acquire a terracotta figure, or an interesting fragment of one, dating from the days of the Roman Empire, or a Greek bowl decorated with figures – red-on-black or black-on-red – of the 5th century BC, and they need cost no more, perhaps even less, than a Victorian porcelain vase in dubious taste. **80**

Persian

Much the same may be said of Persian pottery of the classic period, 12th to 14th centuries AD. It is decorated sometimes with golden lustre, sometimes with enamel colours – blue, purple, red and green – and has a subdued, matt appearance which shows to its best advantage in shallow bowls. A splendid collection might also be made of the tiles with decoration in relief, depicting animals, birds and foliage, and bearing inscriptions.

'Tin-glazed' Wares – Majolica, Faience, Delft

Persian influence is very noticeable on some of the early Italian pottery, for example, the dry-jug jar with concave sides called *albarello* which is representative of a very wide range of such pots, made of a soft-bodied earthenware covered with a lead glaze to which oxide of tin was added and decorated in a variety of colours (polychrome) or blue only on a whitish ground. As well as apothecaries' drug-jars, dishes, ewers, vases and other vessels were made in many countries and decorated in the same sort of way.

The Italian version is known as *Majolica* owing to an early misunderstanding. Spanish-Moorish pottery of the same basic type as the Italian, but with a metallic lustre decoration, was brought into Italy from Valencia on Majorcan ships, giving rise to the belief that it was made in Majorca. The name *Majolica* has stuck to this day.

Between 1450 and 1630, the finest Italian Majolica was made at Urbino, Venice, Genoa and Faenza, richly painted with trophies, arabesques, figures and flowers in a brilliant range of colours. This varied palette was forced into disuse by competition from the blue-and-white Chinese porcelain that was now coming into Europe, and which the Western potters had to imitate in order to survive. The sculptor della Robbia helped to raise pottery to the level of fine art.

French *faience* has much in common with Majolica, borrowing its name from Faenza. It was made at a number of centres, the work of Rouen and Nevers in the late 17th and early 18th centuries being distinguished by bold modelling of such things as tureens, and confidently painted designs, both in colour and in blue-and-white. The French tradition dates from about 1550, when *Henri II* ware was made at St Porchaire, involving a process of inlaying coloured enamels into a layer of pipe-

clay on a light body. Unfortunately few genuine pieces survive. Almost as rare are the early plates made by Bernard Palissy, decorated in a slightly unpleasant way with serpents and toads. Many naïve collectors imagine they have found a piece of Palissy ware, ornamented in this way, when what they really have is a nasty bit of 19th century Portuguese pottery. French faience, with an agreeable peasant flavour, has continued to be made at Quimper and elsewhere down to the present day.

Delft, in Holland, was devoted to the brewing of beer until about 1600, when its people's loyalties became divided between beer and *tin-glazed* pottery. The industry was highly organized into a guild which imposed strict rules of entry on its members, maintained high standards and kept a record of potters' marks which has come down to us, making the attribution of Dutch

Delft that much easier. However, copies, complete with mark, abound. Most of the wares were inspired by oriental porcelain brought in by the Dutch East India Company. Similar wares were made elsewhere in Holland and, indeed, in most European countries. In England, it was made at Bristol, Lambeth and Fulham in London, Liverpool, and at Wincanton in Somerset. There was also at least one factory in Ireland. It all goes by the slightly confusing name, *English Delftware*. **81** Large dishes are the most usual things encountered, with spirited decoration in blue or in colours – yellow, purple, green. Subjects are *chinoiseries*, flowers, Adam

81 *English Delftware jug with the arms of the Apothecaries Co inscribed on it, dated 1650.*

82 *A kreussen stone ware tankard of cylindrical shape.*

71

83 *Rhenish stoneware jug, mounted in silver gilt.*

84 *Pottery group by Obadiah Sherratt. Hector Munro carried off by a tiger.*

and Eve, patriotic if crude portraits of William of Orange and, in the mid-18th century, inscriptions on punch bowls proclaiming 'Success to British Arms'.

Stoneware

In Germany, the use of soft-bodied, lead-glazed or tin-enamelled pottery was largely restricted to stoves and tiles. **82** A much harder ware, glazed by throwing salt into the kiln, was made at Cologne and elsewhere from about 1540, being used especially for wine jugs with 'grey-beard' masks – popularly supposed to satirize Cardinal Bellarmin and known still as '*Bellarmines*'. These

were exported to England and elsewhere, complete with Rhenish wine; the earliest were white, the later ones brown, and the latest of all were grey with blue decoration.

English potters were stimulated to compete with them, and *tiger ware* jugs with a brown-and-yellow glaze were made in the Elizabethan period. When mounted in silver of the period, they command high prices. By about 1670, John Dwight of Fulham had produced stoneware of a very high order, hardened by the inclusion of calcined flint, which he mistakenly claimed to be *hard-paste* porcelain. Busts modelled in this material are very beautiful but also very rare. Much more common are the Fulham jugs, made on the lines of the German ones and sometimes decorated with the initials and portraits of Charles II or William III. The plainer

ones are difficult to distinguish from the contemporary German product, but an expert can tell a great deal by examining the marks on the base left by the potter's wheel.

Two Dutchmen, the Elers brothers, introduced salt-glazed stoneware into Staffordshire at the end of the 17th century, and also made an unglazed, close-grained, red stoneware of a kind used by the Chinese for teapots, which the Staffordshire potters copied.

There is a legend to the effect that John Astbury, who became one of the greatest potters of the early 18th century, learned much from the Elers by obtaining employment with them and pretending to be a dullard. Industrial spying of this kind was a regular feature of pottery and porcelain manufacture in those days. Later, he brought white clay from the West Country to Staf-

fordshire, added ground flint to it and made a fine, white, salt-glazed stoneware, used extensively for useful and decorative wares, and easily distinguished from lead-glazed wares by its texture, which is a little rough – often likened to the feel of orange-skin. **85** It was used on many of the early Staffordshire figures.

Josiah Wedgwood used stoneware in a highly sophisticated way for his black basalt ware *(Egyptian porcelain)* produced first in 1766, and used both for tea-table wares in classical, silver shapes, and for medallions, library busts and figures. **87** This has no glaze, as such, though it is sometimes seen flecked with a metallic glint to heighten the similarity to bronze, and vases were painted with enamel colours.

Jasperware – the product for which Wedgwood is best known – was also a kind of stoneware, again with-

out glaze. **90** Classical figures stand out in white relief on a matt ground in various shades of blue, lavender, green and black. First perfected in 1775, these colours penetrated right through the background, but from about 1780 the stains were sometimes applied only to the surface (*Jasper-dip*).

Stone china was a toughened earthenware first produced in Staffordshire about 1805 as an economic rival to porcelain. Mason of Lane Delph patented his formula for *Ironstone China'* in 1813, and dinner-services, jugs with snake handles and other objects are still produced, bearing the mark in full. **91** This type of ware was, in spite of the patent, made at many other factories both in England and America. Duche of Savannah is believed to have made it as early as about 1740, but the period 1850-1900 is the one in which American makers produced vast quantities, calling it *opaque porcelain* or *flint china*. Regardless of name, the body is always much the same, and the glaze is always a lead glaze.

Creamware

This was an improved earthenware, very light in weight, the body pale in colour and the lead glaze creamy, which was produced in Staffordshire about the middle of the 18th century. From 1760, it posed a serious threat to makers of porcelain and Continental faience – particularly French. Wedgwood made a version that became known as *Queen's Ware* and Leeds is celebrated for delicately modelled vases, mugs and other useful and ornamental objects. Creamware was often left undecorated, but some pieces were painted with enamel colours.

It was made extensively in America from about 1770, first at Charlestown and shortly after at Salem,

North Carolina. Several factories for its manufacture were set up in Philadelphia in the 1790s, New York and Pittsburgh were to follow, with Louisville and Kentucky producing the last fine creamware between 1830 and 1838. The final significant attempt was that of the Shaker colony at Amana, Iowa, which produced some rather coarse wares between 1850 and 1890.

Redware

From about 1625, the American colonists at Jamestown had made simple crocks – pitchers, milk-pans, bowls, mugs, plates – from common red clay: '*peasant*-*style*' pottery, for which the New England clay proved ideal. These functional pots are often gaily splashed with colour, and continued to be made long after the Revolution had removed official English prohibition on colonial manufacturing. Certainly as late as 1840, the Zoarites – a religious sect in the Mid-West – were making porringers, pitchers and wash-bowls for sale to the farmers of Ohio.

Transfer-printing

There are many ways of decorating pottery; one which revolutionized the trade was invented at Battersea in London about 1753, and was soon in extensive use at Worcester and Liverpool. A design was engraved on a copper plate which was then inked, so that it could be printed on to a tissue and, while still wet, transferred to the piece of pottery. Early transfers were in black, on to the glaze, and slightly later, in blue, under the glaze. The method was used on a vast amount of lead-glazed pottery, the ubiquitous Willow Pattern being a characteristic example.

85 *Two salt glaze bear jugs circa 1740.*

86 *Zebra and snake, circa 1860. The Staffordshire potteries made splendid figures of imaginary combats between animals, for sale outside the fairground menageries.*

87 *An early impressed-marked Spode Basalt teapot of the 1790s or even 1780s.*

88 *Deruta majolica dish, circa 1620-30.*

88

91 *Representative pieces from an early Mason's Ironstone Dessert Service, decorated with a typical 'Japan' pattern, circa 1815-20.*

92 *An unusual pair of 'comforter' dogs with puppies. Staffordshire circa 1860.*

93 *Martinware, grotesque spoon warmer.*

94 *Martinware figures of birds, made as Tobacco jars.*

91

92

93

94

Victorian Pottery

As the industrialization of the Staffordshire potteries developed in the 19th century, much hand-work was replaced by mass-production methods. **92** The figures produced in moulds from the middle of the century to its end, many of them representing popular celebrities, illustrate the decline from the earlier work of Astbury, Whieldon, Walton and the Wood family. These *named* Staffordshire figures are nevertheless much sought after today.

Salt-glazed stoneware was revived by Doulton's of Lambeth, and one of their modellers, Martin, together with his two brothers, broke fresh ground with vases formed as grotesque animals. **94** William de Morgan, a member of the idealistic group led by William Morris, set up a kiln in the garden of his Chelsea home which developed into a commercial proposition, producing wares decorated with brilliantly coloured glazes, the secret of which had long lain dormant and which he re-discovered.

Many amateurs – women especially – became interested in pottery and its decoration in the mid-19th century, and by about 1890, some 10,000 women in America alone were busily making or decorating ceramics of various kinds, about half of them earning a living as decorators.

PORCELAIN

95

95 Hard-paste porcelain plate, painted in the enamel colours of the famille verte. Inscribed with birthday wishes probably for the Emperor. Chinese; reign of K'ang Hsi (1662-1722)

96 Plate, soft-paste porcelain, painted in enamel colours. The subject is taken from an engraving 'Bocconia' forming plate IV of Plantae Selectae, published by Dr Christopher James Trew, in parts between 1755 and 1773. English (Chelsea); about 1755.

96

97 Hard-paste porcelain teapot, painted in enamel colours and gilt. Marks: 'KPM' and crossed swords in underglaze-blue, and '55' in gold. German (Meissen), about 1724.

97

98 *Hard-paste porcelain cup and saucer, painted in enamel colours with a European design, perhaps by Boucher. Chinese; mid-18th century.*

99 *Hard-paste porcelain lion, painted in enamel colours. Kakiemon style. Japanese (Arita, Hizen province); late 17th century.*

100 *Figure of Pantaloon from the Commedia dell' Arte. Hard-paste porcelain painted in enamel colours. Modelled by Franz Anton Bustelli. German (Nymphenburg); about 1760.*

99

Chinese Porcelain

Although the Chinese potters had been acquainted with china-clay since the Han dynasty (206 BC – 220 AD), it was not until the T'ang dynasty (about 850 AD) that knowledge of china-stone enabled them to make a ceramic body that was both white and translucent, and it was during the Sung dynasty (960-1279-AD) that some of the most beautiful Chinese wares were made. Ting ware, made in North East China, often has a moulded design emphasized by the typical ivory-coloured glaze. Two other types of porcelain, made slightly later in the Sung dynasty, were the *Lung-ch'uan* and *Ching-pai* wares. The first was a near-white body under a bluish-green translucent glaze (celadon), which showed to advantage the incised, or moulded decoration. The second were delicately formed wares, that were made in the Kiangsi province, which became the centre of Chinese porcelain manufacture. They were distinguished by the pale-blue glaze, and were decorated with incised designs of flowers and foliage.

Ming Dynasty

After 1279, when the Sung dynasty was overthrown by the Mongols, fashions changed, and during the entire Ming dynasty (1368-1644) the potters paid attention to painted designs rather than to form, and achieved great success by painting in underglaze-blue directly on to the body of the ware, prior to glazing.

The dish with yellow ground was made during the reign of the Emperor Chêng Te (1506-21 AD) when the art of fusing enamels, or coloured glass, on to the surface of the glaze was perfected.

Ch'ing or Manchu Dynasty

During the reign of the Emperor K'ang Hsi (1662-1722) the flourishing centre of Ching-tê-Chên reached its peak and produced in addition to numerous wares for Court use, large quantities of porcelain to satisfy the demands of the European market. The plate shown in Plate **95** is of exceptional beauty, and was probably made to celebrate the birthday of the Emperor towards the end of his reign, for the style of decoration is more typical of the reign of the next Emperor, Yung Chêng (1723-35).

Especially popular during the reign of K'ang Hsi was a range of wares called *famille verte* which were all in a range of colours in which various shades of green predominate. The enamel colours were often painted directly on to the porcelain body, rather than on to the glaze. In the case of the vase shown in the introduction a

100

black enamel background has been used, giving rise to the name *famille noire*, and later rose-pink enamels – *famille rose* – were dominant throughout the reign of Ch'ien Lung (1726-95), and especially used on wares made to order for the European market. Some of these were decorated with coats-of-arms, but by the second quarter of the 18th century many pictorial designs were being copied from French prints or drawings. **98** Most of the enamel decoration was added to the porcelain at Canton, where all the actual trading was carried out. The Chinese decorators had great difficulty in painting European faces and invariably all the characters, whatever nationality, have an Oriental look. Punch-bowls, with pictures of ships or fox-hunts were especially in demand in England during the middle of the 18th century, and command very high prices today.

Japanese Porcelain

The potters of Japan appear to have made very little true porcelain prior to the early part of the 17th century, when they discovered the necessary clay deposits in Hizen, and made wares painted in purple-toned underglaze-blue, on a greyish-coloured body. The later wares, popular in Europe, were the large dishes and sets of five vases painted in rich vermilion and other colours, and decorated with jumbles of flowers and profuse gilding – a style known as Imari, the name of the seaport from where the porcelains of Arita were shipped.

Some of the finest Japanese porcelains are those decorated in the Kakiemon style, named after a family of Arita potters credited with the introduction, about the middle of the 17th century, of enamel painting in soft reds, greenish-blue, turquoise, yellow and occasional

underglaze-blue. **99**

Entirely different are the porcelains of Kutani dating from about 1660. The painting is powerful and seemingly careless, with strong greens, blues, dull yellows, rich purples and a dark, opaque red. Many later Kutani wares are almost completely covered with these enamels. Nabeshima was a prince who established a porcelain factory near Arita about 1660. The soft blue lies under a smooth, flawless glaze, the enamel painted flowers and foliage often showing a geometrical precision. The porcelain made for the Prince of Hirado, from about 1712, is usually of a perfect, clear, white quality, upon which the soft, violet-toned, blue landscapes with figure-subjects show to great advantage.

101 *Group of two figures, soft-paste porcelain, painted in enamel colours. Italian (Capodimonte); about 1750.*

102 *Ewer and basin, soft-paste porcelain, painted in enamel colours. Mark: interlaced 'L's enclosing 'K', the date letter for 1763, also interlaced 'S's in blue enamel, the latter being the mark of Catrice, the painter. Perhaps the 'pot à l'eau jaune, enfants camayeux' supplied to the Duc d'Orléans, in 1764.*

103 *Figure of glazed white hard-paste porcelain. Austrian (Vienna, Du Paquier's factory); about 1720.*

GERMANY

Meissen

When Augustus II, King of Poland, succeeded to the title of Elector of Saxony in 1694, one of the first demands he made of his economic adviser Von Tschirnhaus, was for an organized survey of the country's mineral wealth in the hope of finding the materials necessary for making, firstly fine glass, and secondly hard-paste porcelain of the Chinese type.

In 1704 JF Böttger, a young alchemist who had rashly claimed to be able to conjure gold from base metal, was placed under the supervision of Tschirnhaus. By 1707 they had between them produced a very fine red stoneware, and in the following year the first white porcelain was produced at Meissen. It was nearer 1720 before Böttger used china stone together with china-clay, to produce an even whiter porcelain than the Chinese – the first hard-paste porcelain made in Europe.

From 1720 a brilliant young painter, JG Höroldt helped to produce the many copies and pastiches of oriental wares so sought after by Augustus. **97** Under Höroldt, Meissen prospered and the famous crossed-swords, adopted as a factory-mark in 1723 became known throughout the world.

In 1727 a young Dresden sculptor, JG Kirchner was engaged to model large animals and vases but was finally replaced in 1733 by the famous JJ Kaendler, who was favoured by the chief minister von Bruhl. Kaendler was now requested to design table-wares decorated with high-relief and figure modelling, such as the Swan Service made for Bruhl himself, comprising 2,200 pieces, decorated with swans, marine deities, mermaids and shells. But he is probably better known for his series of small figures modelled after the characters of the Italian Comedy, Harlequin and Pantaloon being the most popular.

For many years Meissen enjoyed a near monopoly of hard-paste porcelain manufacture in Europe, but it became increasingly difficult to keep the secrets of production safe, and many rival factories were to start, among them Höchst, Nymphenburg and Frankenthal. **100** Meissen finally lost its place as the fashion-setter for European porcelain during the Seven Years War (1756-63), when the factory was occupied by the troops of Frederick the Great. However, it was during this time that the centrepiece was made as part of a large dinner-service for General von Mollendorf. **104**

VIENNA

Du Paquier had endeavoured to produce hard-paste porcelain in Vienna from 1717, but it was not until he persuaded Stölzel, the kiln-master from Meissen, to join him, that he was really successful. His earliest wares often had a bluish-grey body with a slightly smokey-coloured glaze. The Oriental figure is a very rare and early example of Viennese porcelain, which during the

104 *Centrepiece from a Dinner-Service. German (Meissen); 1761. Hard-paste porcelain painted in enamel colours and gilt. The group of* Silenus on the Ass, *and the figures of satyrs were modelled by Johann Joachim Kaendler. The large service was made to the order of Frederick the Great for the Prussian General Wichard Joachim Heinrich von Mollendorf.*

105 *Teapot and Cover, hard-paste porcelain decorated with underglaze-blue transfer-prints and stencilling. Italian (Doccia); about 1740-50.*

Du Paquier period consisted mostly of fine table-wares of extreme baroque forms, decorated with enamel scrollwork, shell-like palmettes and intricate, lattice-like gilding. **103** The mark – a shield with two bars – was adopted at the beginning of the State Period (1744-84), during which the wares were more often fashioned after those of Meissen, as can be seen in the figures of shepherds, vendors, waiters, musicians, etc. From 1784, under the management of Sorgenthal, Viennese potters endeavoured to re-capture the forms of classical antiquity, and often tended to over-decorate. The original factory closed in 1866, but the mark has since been used by others.

ITALY

Florence

The first European country to become conversant with Chinese porcelain was almost certainly Italy, and it was there that the earliest attempts to imitate such wares were made. Credit for the first manufacture of a soft-paste (artificial) porcelain goes to the concern set up by the Grand Duke Francesco I de'Medici in 1575, which continued until his death in 1587, seemingly just to serve the needs of the family, rather than as a commercial enterprise.

The factory founded in 1735 at Doccia, near Florence, by Carlo Ginori continues to this day under the name of Richard Ginori, and a typical product is the teapot shown in plate. **105** It is of the early paste, which is hard and grey in comparison with the contemporary Meissen. The baroque-like snake-spout and the high domed lid are often seen on the early wares. Overfiring often resulted in the glaze taking on the 'orange-peel' texture, normally associated with salt-glaze stoneware.

Between about 1770 and 1790 the grey body was often disguised by using a glaze made both white and opaque by the addition of tin-oxide, a type of glaze more familiar on earthenware. It was at Doccia that the fashion originated for Bacchanalian scenes in low relief – a style often copied on late 19th century German wares, fraudulently marked with a crowned 'N'.

Naples

The Capodimonte factory was established near Naples by Charles of Bourbon in 1743, and continued there until it was transferred to Buen Retiro near Madrid, in 1759, where it survived until 1800. The mark at both places is always the *fleur-de-lys*, either impressed or painted in blue or gilt; never a crowned *N*, which was the

106 *Figure of a musician, soft-paste porcelain, painted in enamel colours. Marks: a large 'A' in underglaze-blue and an anchor and dagger in red enamel. English (Bow); about 1765.*

107 *Bone-china plate, painted in enamel colours and gilt. Pattern-plate for a service made for King William IV, whose arms are in the centre. Mark: a griffin, the crest of the Earl Fitzwilliam and 'Royal Rock'. Works, Brameld, printed in crimson. English (Swinton, Yorkshire); about 1830.*

108 *Soft-paste porcelain Jardinière, with opaque tin-glaze, painted in enamel colours in Kakiemon style. Mark: a hunting horn in red. French (Chantilly); about 1725-50.*

107

mark of the Royal Naples factory founded later in 1771. The beauty of Capodimonte porcelain is best seen on the many figures modelled by Gricci – lovers, Italian Comedy characters and fisherfolk, together with religious subjects. **101**

FRANCE

Saint-Cloud

Pierre Chicaneau experimented with the manufacture of soft-paste porcelain at Saint-Cloud and his family improved upon his discoveries until, by 1693, they were able to claim that their wares equalled those of the Far East. Their wares were seldom large and were usually heavily potted, but were of a quality that warranted the Paris merchants enhancing them with addition of fine *ormolu* (gilt-bronze). The factory survived until 1766.

Chantilly

In 1725 Ciquaire Cirou established a soft-paste porcelain factory here, under the patronage of the Prince de Conde, a great lover of Japanese porcelain decorated in the *Kakiemon* style (see Japan), and some of the finest wares produced at Chantilly from about 1725-40 were made in imitation of it. This style of decoration required a whiter porcelain than was available, and so tin-oxide was added to the glaze to hide the creamy soft-paste body. **108** These styles were replaced about 1750 by natural flower-painting on a clear glaze of the Meissen type, and later still the vogue was for decoration in blue, either underglaze or enamel, and often showed the popular *Chantilly sprig*. The original factory closed about 1800, but other concerns continued well into the 19th century, all using the original factory-mark of a hunting-horn, sometimes with the initials of the proprietor.

Mennecy

Some of the most beautiful soft-paste porcelain ever produced was made at Mennecy from 1734. The paste is a milky-white, the glaze *wet* and brilliant; the colours, which seem to sink into the glaze, include rose-pinks, bright blues and brownish-greens. Particularly pleasing are the groups of children, obviously inspired by the painting of Boucher. The most common Mennecy mark is the initials 'DV' (for the patron, duc de Villeroy), sometimes in red or blue enamel, but more often incised. **110**

Vincennes & Sèvres

The factory was started in 1738 in a royal chateau at Vincennes, moving to a new building at Sèvres in 1756. Despite the early start it was nearer 1749 before good quality wares were being produced in any quantity. Due to the high cost of production, the factory might have closed down in 1759 if Madame de Pompadour had not persuaded King Louis XV to purchase the factory himself. Up until about 1770 all Sèvres porcelain was made from a soft-paste, but from about 1772 this gradually gave way to true porcelain, soft-paste being finally abandoned about 1804.

The history of Sèvres is well documented, including the dates when the various coloured grounds were first introduced, the names of the painters and gilders, the type of decoration they specialized in, and the years they were employed. About 1750, the factory adopted the royal cipher (crossed 'L's) as a mark and from 1753 the letters of the alphabet were used to indicate the year, starting with 'A' in 1753 and ending with 'PP' in 1793, when the concern was taken over by the Republic. (Forgeries are frequently marked with the letter 'A'.)

The *pastille burner* has the early, ground-colour of *bleu celeste*, first introduced in 1752. The yellow (*jaune jonquille*) **102** followed in 1753, pea-green in 1756, and the powdery pink of *rose Pompadour* in 1757. The authenticity of a piece of Sèvres porcelain can quite often be judged by the quality of the gilding which, on genuine 18th century examples, is usually outstanding.

As early as 1753, a Paris merchant was advertising groups of figures in biscuit-porcelain. **109** The French were the first to leave their figures in this unglazed and undecorated state, a fashion later adopted at the English factory of Derby. The firm of Samson of Paris that was established in 1845 made many copies of Sèvres biscuit-

110 Milk-jug and cover, soft-paste porcelain, painted in enamel colours. Mark: 'DV' incised. French (Mennecy); mid-18th century.

figures, but their mark usually was of interlaced 'S's in diamond form. Samson copied the work of many factories, and some of these decorative reproductions are now collected in their own right.

ENGLAND, WALES AND NORTHERN IRELAND

Chelsea

Porcelain was not made in England until about 1745, when the Huguenot silversmith, Nicholas Sprimont, began to make soft-paste porcelain at Chelsea, in London, probably assisted initially by a Charles Gouyn, a jeweller. Chelsea falls conveniently into five distinct periods, four of which are known by the mark in use at the time, though much was unmarked. The earliest, known as the *incised triangle*, dating from about 1745-49, is found on wares of a glassy soft-paste, with a good, clear glaze which rarely crazed. Many of the early shapes were similar to those previously made by Sprimont in silver, taking the form of small jugs, salts, sauce-boats, etc.

From about 1749-52, the mark of an anchor, raised in relief on an oval medallion, was used. In this and the following red-anchor period (circa 1752-8), the glaze usually looks distinctly whiter, due to the addition of a small quantity of tin-oxide. The designs were very rarely original, imitating first Meissen, and then Sèvres. The tureen in the form of a rabbit **116** is a copy of Meissen, and reminds us of the love of naturalism at the table in the German Courts.

The table-wares of Chelsea can often be identified, irrespective of mark, by three little blemishes left in the glaze by the stilts used to support the wares in the kiln. Tears of glaze which sometimes formed on the edge of the foot-rims, were often ground away, giving a characteristic *ground foot-rim*. *Red-anchor* plates, when held against a strong light, exhibit tiny *moons* of greater translucency than the rest.

During the years 1758-70 the majority of Chelsea wares were marked with a gold anchor – only too frequently seen on hard-paste Continental reproduction of Chelsea. In 1770 the Chelsea concern was taken over by William Duesbury, already proprietor of the Derby factory, who continued to run both until 1784, when Chelsea was finally closed.

Bow

The actual site of the Bow porcelain factory is now known to have been situated just beyond the boundaries of London, in Essex. Although early patents were taken out in 1744, it was probably about 1747 before soft-paste porcelain was being made in commerical quantities.

At their peak, Bow employed about 300 hands, mostly engaged in the making of wares decorated in the blue-and-white Chinese style. Their figures lacked the sophistication of those produced at Chelsea, but possessed a naïve charm of their own. **106** Knowledge of technical methods aids identification. To produce their porcelain figures, the Chelsea workmen poured slip or watered-down clay, into the hollow plaster-of-Paris moulds, whereas at Bow, the clay was used in a dough-like condition, and pressed into the walls of the moulds by hand. The Bow factory was taken over, and closed, by William Duesbury of Derby in 1776.

Derby

Prior to the establishment of a Derby porcelain factory by William Duesbury in 1756, a number of very interesting and rare pieces were made by André Planché, usually superior to the early wares of Duesbury's factory, where figures were given a Meissen-like appearance, not so apparent in vases, etc. **114**

The Derby factory did not adopt the regular factory-mark of a crown, crossed batons and 'D' until about 1782. During the *Chelsea-Derby* period, many of their table-wares were marked with an anchor and 'D', either side-by-side, or in monogram form. This marking was very inconsistent and the bowl in plate **115** is still marked with a simple Chelsea-like gold anchor, despite the late date of 1779.

Many fine painters were employed at Derby, one of the best being Zachariah Boreman, who specialized

III

in painting the Derbyshire countryside. **112** Robert Bloor took over the factory in 1811, reviving so-called Imari patterns with brassy gilding on a glaze which often crazed. The original Derby factory closed in 1848, the present-day Royal Derby Porcelain Company being established in 1876.

Worcester

The Worcester porcelain factory was established in the mid-18th century, and is still in production today. A partnership was formed in 1751 which took over the factory of Lund and Miller of Bristol, who produced a fine soft-paste porcelain from 1748-52. Recent discoveries suggest that it is very difficult to separate the unmarked wares of Lund's Bristol and early Worcester.

Worcester porcelain was usually of a very high quality, capable of standing sudden changes of temperature without cracking or crazing. Apart from a small number of figures, produced about 1770, their output in the 18th century consisted of table-wares and decorative vases, many of which were decorated in only underglaze-blue. About 1765, they began to employ colour in a somewhat similar fashion to Chelsea potters of the *gold-anchor* period. Much celebrated are the *exotic birds* painted in *reserves* of clear porcelain against a ground of scale-blue, pink, yellow or green. The work of the early 19th century was highly decorated and is now much sought after.

Caughley

Thomas Turner acquired his knowledge of porcelain manufacture while working at the Worcester factory. About 1772 he started to manufacture his own wares at Caughley (pronounced Calf-ley), which were very similar to those of Worcester. Many pieces of Caughley were sent to the decorating establishment of Chamberlain at Worcester, where they were painted with exotic birds. Caughley was taken over by John Rose of Coalport in 1799, who also produced a *hard-*

111 *Teapot and cover, hard-paste porcelain moulded in relief and covered with a lustrous glaze. Irish (Belleek); about 1865.*

112 *Teapot from a cabaret service, soft-paste porcelain, painted in enamel colours and gilt. Mark: 'D' under a crown, crossed batons with six dots in blue enamel. On the base is inscribed in blue, 'On the Trent, Derbyshire'. English (Derby); about 1790.*

112

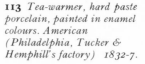

113 *Tea-warmer, hard paste porcelain, painted in enamel colours. American (Philadelphia, Tucker & Hemphill's factory) 1832-7.*

114 *Vase, soft-paste porcelain, painted in enamel colours. English (Derby); about 1755-6.*

115 *Soft-paste porcelain punch bowl, painted in enamel colours and gilt. Inside are the arms of the Cooper's Company of London. Mark: an anchor in gold. English (Derby); dated 1779.*

116 *Soft-paste porcelain tureen and cover, painted in natural colours. Mark: inside tureen, an anchor, inside tureen and cover, 'No. 1' all in red. English (Chelsea); about 1755.*

114

115

paste porcelain, much of which, until recently, was thought to have been made at New Hall in Staffordshire.

Plymouth, Bristol and New Hall

The secret of *hard-paste* porcelain, that in England had proved so elusive, was discovered independently by William Cookworthy of Plymouth in 1768. He moved to Bristol in 1770, where production was continued until 1781, when the patent was sold to a group of potters to form New Hall. The earliest Plymouth porcelain sometimes showed technical defects, but under Richard Champion, who took over the Bristol factory in about 1773, these were corrected. Most table-wares and vases were very elaborate, in the styles popular at Sèvres. Figures, such as the Four Seasons, often have rocky bases.

The hard-paste porcelain made at New Hall was somewhat different and appears to have a softer glaze than that originally used at Plymouth and Bristol. From 1812 New Hall went over to the manufacture of bone-china until closing in 1835.

Spode

The second Josiah Spode, of Stoke-on-Trent, Staffordshire, perfected a formula for a typically English compromise between hard- and soft-paste porcelain, about 1794. This became the standard product, known as *bone china*, because of the high content of bone-ash. The firm was extremely successful, making useful and decorative wares of all kinds, from the simplest blue-and-white to elaborate patterns like the famous '1166' – richly decorated with gilt scaling.

After Spode's lifetime, the factory passed to Cope-land and Garrett (1833-47) and WT Copeland and Sons ran it from then until the present day. They are credited with being the first to perfect Parian ware – white body, like biscuit porcelain but with a marble-like sheen – used for statuary figures and busts. Similar work was produced in America.

Coalport, Rockingham and Minton

Coalport in Shropshire, and Rockingham at Swinton in Yorkshire made wares in keeping with the fashion for *revived rococo* in the second quarter of the 19th century. **107** Rockingham were inconsistent in the use of their *griffin* mark, but we now know that they did not make all the cottages, or figures of poodles with 'shaggy' coats, popularly attributed to them. The Rockingham factory ceased in 1842, whereas wares are still being made in Staffordshire today under the name of 'Coalport'.

The factory of Thomas Minton is also still in existence today. Starting in 1793, their wares have always been of a high quality. During recent years, the management have made their early pattern-books available for research, and many wares formerly thought to be Coalbrookdale, or *Staffordshire*, can now be identified with certainty as Minton.

Belleek

The hard-paste porcelains made at Belleek, Northern Ireland have now become collectors' pieces, although the factory was not established until 1860. The porcelain is a Parian-like body with a *mother-of-pearl* iridescent glaze. Their designers were very much under the spell of the sea, using marine plants and shells for most models. **111**

AMERICAN

The first mention of porcelain-making in America was in 1739, six years prior to the establishment of the Chelsea factory in England – and it concerns Andrew Duché, of Savannah, but no porcelain produced by him has ever been identified with certainty. The same is true of John Bartlam, an 'insolvent master potter' from England, who went to South Carolina hoping to make true porcelain, in about 1770.

Bonnin and Morris

The first success appears to have been at the factory set up in about 1769 in Philadelphia by Gousse Bonnin and George Morris, who claimed their productions were equal to those of the factory in 'Box (Bow) near London'. The group of wares now attributed to Bonnin and Morris are of a thickly potted soft-paste porcelain decorated in underglaze-blue.

The best example is a centrepiece formed by four shell-shaped dishes, very much akin to Bow. This and a sauce-boat are now in the Brooklyn Museum. Both are marked with what appears to be a small '*p*' in underglaze-blue. Due to financial difficulties the factory was forced to close in 1772.

Tucker

Philadelphia was also the city where William Ellis Tucker first produced a hard-paste porcelain in 1826 for which he won awards in 1827, 1828 and 1831. After his death in 1832 the concern was run by a Judge Joseph Hemphill, with Thomas Tucker as manager. It closed in 1838.

The porcelain was very similar in both form and decoration to that being produced in France during the same period and consisted almost entirely of table-wares, vases, and pitchers. The enamel painting of flowers and landscapes was of a very high quality, as were the romantic scenes painted in sepia and *charcoal*. Many vases, pitchers and dishes were decorated solely with finely applied gilding, sometimes including inscriptions and dates.

Bennington

The factory of Christopher W Fenton at Bennington, Vermount, produced Parian ware, similar to that made by Copeland in England, in about 1847, including the famous Greek Slave modelled by Hiram Powers. Blue-and-white porcelain and more rarely, tan or green-and-white, was made from 1851. The mark USP *(United States Porcelain)* occurs on pieces made from 1853-8, when the factory closed.

Greenpoint

There were two factories in what is now Brooklyn. The first, owned by Cartlidge & Co (1848-56) employed Josiah Jones as a modeller of portrait busts in unglazed porcelain, the subjects being celebrated Americans such as General Zachary Taylor and Daniel Webster. They also made many novelties – buttons, chessmen, and cameos.

Boch and Brother began in 1850, making door knobs and table-ware in bone china. TC Smith took over in 1861, called it the Union Porcelain works and began to make hard-paste porcelain in about 1864. The symbol of a bird's head was not added to the factory mark until 1876, by which date Karl Müller was modelling heads of the great poets.

MINIATURES
& SILHOUETTES

117 *Left to right, top row: enamel miniature of a lady by CF Zincke, early 18th century; Mrs Lowndes Stone by Richard Crosse, last quarter of the 18th century; enamel miniature of a gentleman, by CF Zincke, early 18th century.*

Centre: an officer by Patrick McMorland, last quarter of the 18th century; General Sir Archibald Campbell, KCB, of Inverneill, by John Smart, signed and dated 1786-1 (India); an officer, by Jeremiah Meyer, last quarter of the 18th century.

Bottom: a lady, by Andrew Plimer, circa 1800; a gentleman, by Samuel Cooper, signed, mid-17th century; a lady, by Sampson Towgood Roch, signed and dated 1798.

118 *A lady by Andrew Plimer.*

119 *Sir Kenelm Digby by Peter Oliver.*

120 *A lady by George Engleheart.*

118

119

120

BRITISH PORTRAIT MINIATURES

It is doubtful if portrait miniatures were painted in England before Henry VIII came to the throne in 1509. Because of his love for art and culture, Henry invited artists from the Continent to come to England, among them Hans Holbein in 1526. There was, however, great Continental interest in the development of painting in miniature, and because of this it was difficult for the English to examine to any great depth the techniques employed by foreign artists, apart from the piecing together of scrappy biographical allusions, references and accounts. Much more is known about the methods of English 16th century miniature painting, firstly, through the examination of existing miniatures, and secondly, because Hilliard, who based his methods on Holbein, wrote a treatise on the subject called *The Art of Limning*.

Nicholas Hilliard (154?-1619) was the first great English-born miniature painter. Fortunately, a large number of his works exists, although there are the inevitable few that were probably painted by his anonymous pupils. Among the immediate followers of Hilliard was a pupil, Isaac Oliver, who together with his son, Peter Oliver, formed the great link between the 16th and 17th centuries. Although Oliver was a Frenchman of Huguenot descent, he holds an important place in the development of English miniature painting.

With the exception of portraits in oils, for which copper was used as a surface, watercolour miniatures were painted either on vellum or parchment until the 18th century. The vellum, being thin, was stretched over a piece of card for support (it was usually a playing card), which not only could be found easily, but was also suitably strong to offer support. Having prepared the medium, the artist then had to go through the rigours of refining his pigments from their raw state to a condition suitable for use. At this earlier period of painting the preparation required as much care and expertise as the actual ability to apply it.

The history of miniature painting becomes rather clearer in the 17th century as more miniatures have survived. A very long list of artists could be made without too much thought. These include John Hoskins, Samuel and Alexander Cooper, Thomas Flatman, Mary and Charles Beale, and Lawrence Cross. Samuel Cooper (1609-1626/7) is thought by many collectors to be the greatest miniature artist that ever lived. He was certainly a man of genius, and although he was taught the art of miniature painting by his uncle, John Hoskins, he completely broke away from the stylized work produced by his contemporaries.

In the 18th and 19th centuries, colours were already prepared for the artist in powder form. This, together with the use of ivory, which had now been introduced as a surface on which to paint, considerably eased the problems previously faced by the artist.

Although the first recorded use of ivory was as early as 1704, it took some time to be accepted by the profession. But as the 18th century wore on, it gradually replaced vellum, parchment, card and copper. Lawrence Cross on the other hand, who was painting until his death in 1724, never used it at all. Between 1700 and 1750 the use of enamel for portraiture was being used by Boit, Zincke and Rouquet. Although this surface had been used by Petitot and Bordier in the reign of Charles I, since then it had not been common. The gradual improvement of taste and elegance was reflected in the art of the miniature painter, and good work was produced about the middle of the century by artists such as Gervase Spencer, Penelope Cardwardine, Samuel Cotes and Nathaniel Hone.

Until then, nearly all the miniaturists had practised in and around London, but now Dublin and Bath were rapidly becoming fashionable centres too. Dublin had many artists working, and their style became quite distinct. This can be clearly seen in the work by Samuel Collins, George Thinnery, John Commerford and Charles Robertson. Towards the close of the 18th century, Liverpool was becoming a centre for the lesser miniaturists like Thomas Hazlehurst, John and William Hazlitt, John Turmeau and Thomas Hargreaves.

The period of 1765 to 1810 was the time when miniature painting was at its peak. Among the practising artists of this era were people like George Engleheart, Andrew Plimer, Richard Cosway and John Smart. **118** Cosway started his successful career at the age of twelve when he was awarded first prize by the London Society of Artists; Smart, who was then only about eleven, won second prize. Cosway enjoyed a very good clientele and has been on several occasions described as a *Social Dandy*. He was certainly a very colourful character from all accounts, and managed to win the hearts of both Nobility and Royalty. **121** As for Smart, many distinguished people also sat for him, especially Nabobs and Officers employed in the services of the East India Company, when he went to India in 1784. **117**

117

121

121 *Portrait of a Gentleman by Richard Cosway.*

122 *A Miniature of a girl called the Hon. Anne Cadogan by Freese.*

123 *Portrait of a lady by Jeremiah Meyer.*

124 *A silhouette of two gentlemen by August Edouart, signed.*

122

123

The work produced in the early years of the 19th century, though good, was certainly less attractive. The costumes of both men and women were dull and unbecoming. The miniaturist was now using larger pieces of ivory and the rectangle was soon superseded by the oval form. The use of interior and landscape backgrounds became predominant, and although men like Sir William Charles Ross, JCD Engleheart, Anthony Stewart and Alfred Chalon were artists of very high quality, the invention of photography in 1840 quickly overshadowed them.

American Silhouettes

The art of making silhouettes was at its height in England and on the Continent at the end of the 18th and the beginning of the 19th centuries. About the same time silhouettes were becoming most popular in America and artists who crossed the ocean from England in search of fortune and fame in the New World, introduced curious types of machines for tracing the outline and for reproducing the profile to the desired size. This helped to make the portrait quickly and accurately. The small black portraits were known as profile likenesses until August Édouart, the noted French cutter, introduced the word *Silhouette* into the English language in about 1825.

One of the earliest artists to practise in America was Charles Wilson Peale. He was born in Charlestown, Maryland in 1741, and although he received no instruction, he painted several very good works which showed such promise that his friends made arrangements for him to study under Copley in Boston. When he later went to England, he continued his studies under Benja-

98

min West. He returned to America in 1771 and settled in Philadelphia, where he made the art of profilism his profession.

Towards the end of the 18th century, many silhouettists such as Johanna Hale, William Bache, William Doyle, JH Whitcomb, Samuel Folwell, to mention only a few were adopting this new method of portraiture. A little later another superb artist emerged – Master Hubbard. He was an Englishman who began cutting profiles as an infant prodigy. In 1824, at the age of seventeen, he went to New York and finally settled in Philadelphia, where he took lessons from Sully and spent the remainder of his life as a portrait painter. He was tragically killed in 1862 by the explosion of a shell he was filling for the Confederate Army.

The most celebrated silhouettist in America was August Édouart, who was by birth a Frenchman, born in Dunkirk in 1789. Édouart's eventful career started at the age of nineteen when he was placed in charge of a porcelain factory; he then taught for a while and also produced wax models of animals. It was not until his wife died that he started to cut silhouettes with scissors. He would use plain black paper and fold it into two. This enabled him to have an exact duplicate of his work, which he kept himself. From the very beginning he was met with success and visited the fashionable resorts of Bath, Oxford, Cheltenham, Liverpool and Edinburgh. He also spent some time in Dublin and then sailed for America, taking with him his materials and records. Once again, his skill was immediately recognized and he visited Saratoga Springs, Boston, Philadelphia, Washington and New York. Many important people visited his studios, including six Presidents and ex-Presidents, Senators and Orators. **124**

ENGRAVINGS, ETCHINGS
& LITHOGRAPHS

Die Piortenn der Eeren
Vmnd Macht.

The earliest method of print-making was by means of wood-cutting and wood-engraving. On a woodcut the drawing stands out in relief and when inked leaves a black impression, whereas a wood-engraving is carved out leaving the surround in relief to be inked so that a white impression on a black background is obtained. It can readily be seen that both wood-cutting and wood-engraving can be used on the same block – and frequently are, to give the most astonishing effects of *chiaroscuro*.

In the hands of such a master as Albrecht Dürer wood-cutting became a major means of artistic expression, and it particularly lent itself to the expression of the rather morbid, fantastical work produced by the German artists of the period. Another engraver of the time was Lucas Cranach, but his work cannot compare with that of Dürer. **125, 126**

Line-engraving was the principal process used by artists in the 17th and 18th centuries. The drawing is cut in lines with a needle-sharp scoop called a burin on a smooth copper plate, and is then inked so that when paper is pressed on to the plate the impression of the design is transferred to the paper. Many impressions can be taken from the same plate, but since most metal plates tend to wear with use, imperfections creep into the later prints. Consequently most print makers limited, and indeed still limit, even with the refinements of contemporary metal manufacture and printing methods, the edition of any single engraving to a comparatively small number. Variation in texture and shading is achieved by the use of different instruments to cut into the metal.

Hogarth was one of many artists in the 18th century who was well known as an engraver before he made his name as a painter. His famous series on the evils of London was immensely popular and prints of the Harlots' Progress are said to have sold 1,000 copies in the first edition. **127**

Another form of plate engraving, which was used to perfection by Rembrandt, is the etching. The whole plate is covered with some substance impervious to acid and the drawing is made in it. The plate is then submerged in acid which eats into the metal where the substance has been removed, and by recovering the drawing and submerging it several times the artist has far greater means of variation of tone than he has had before. When the process is finished the plate is inked and printed in just the same manner as a burin engraving.

The two most famous of old master etchers are Rembrandt and Goya. **130, 131** Rembrandt's etching of *Christ with the Sick*, printed in 1649, soon became known as the *Hundred-Guilder Print*, for even in Rembrandt's own lifetime it cost that sum of money to buy a copy. He used the medium in the most exciting manner to represent effects of light and shade, and some of his finest etchings are of night scenes or of places in near-darkness, notably *The Adoration of the Shepherds* of 1652. Goya made four main series of etchings during his long career – *Los Caprichos*, a set of eighty black-

126 *Woodcut by Lucas Cranach the Elder of St Anthony tormented by Demons.*

127 *Part of the Rake's Progress by William Hogarth showing the Rose Tavern, Drury Lane. Line Engraving.*

humoured caprices; the eighty-two monumental cries against man's inhumanity to man; *Los Desastros de la Guerra* – The Disasters of War; thirty-three celebrations of bullfighting – *La Tauromaquia*; and eighteen equally black-humoured proverbs – *Los Proverbios*, which are a visual analysis of as many types of folly. In making these etchings, Goya often used a variant on the technique, termed *aquatinting*, when resin is used to cover those parts of the plate which are not cut.

Another variant on the theme of engraving, and one which we shall find to be of particular importance in the development of the late 18th and early 19th century print, is the *mezzotint*. **128** In this process, the engraver works on the plate with rocker and scraper. The rocker stipples the surface of the plate in dots, instead of lines, and the remainder of the unrocked surface is then worked on with scraper and burin. The plate is printed as for an ordinary engraving – with this extremely important difference, that the *crests* made by the stippling pierce the surface of the paper in the printing causing Davenport's memorable phrase 'a certain disintegration of the substance into something distinctly resembling the pile of velvet'.

One more printing method remains to be mentioned – *lithography*. This is a process originally perfected by Alois Senefelder in 1793, and consists of drawing the design upon a stone in greasy crayon or oil-based ink. Water is poured over it and then an oil-based ink which only clings to the greasy drawing; paper is then pressed upon the stone, and a print results. In these days the lithographic stone has been replaced by a zinc plate which for most practical purposes is as effective, and much easier

128 *Mezzotint by Valentine Green of William Innes in the uniform of the Blackheath Golfers, after LF Abbott.*

129 *Stipple engraving entitled 'The Volunteer' by GT Stubbs.*

130 *Aquatint by Francisco Goya:* Los Caprichos, *plate 32.*

131 *Rembrandt's etching of himself in a flat cap.*

to handle than the bulky heavy stones of former times.

All the printing about which we have spoken so far was in black or one-coloured ink on white paper; but early on in the history of print-making, master craftsmen began to experiment with colour. The first English colour-printer recorded was Elisha Kirkhall. In 1724 he printed a two-coloured seascape from a single plate; and four years later made fifty full colour plates after van Huysum to illustrate a book on flowers, John Martyn's *Historia Plantarum Rariorum*, in which he combined etching and mezzotinting in several colours which were then retouched by hand. The other pioneer of colour printing on a principle which is still used today was the Swiss Jacob Christophe Le Blon, who reproduced a picture in full colour in 1711.

All these processes were developed in the 19th century, especially by George Baxter, who combined mezzotint plates with woodblock printing in oiled inks, and made reproductions of any picture so cheaply that he was able to advertize that 'while their artistic beauty may procure for them a place in the Royal palaces throughout Europe the prices at which they are retailed introduces them to the humblest cottages'.

In the United States of America the history of print-making only really begins after the War of Independence – before that most of what little print work there was had been brought over from Europe. There were, of course, exceptions to this general rule. The celebrated Paul Revere made a hand-coloured engraving of *The Boston Massacre* of 1770; and a little later, at the time of the Declaration of Independence, Edward Savage made a series of engraved and mezzotint portraits of famous people including Washington, Franklin and Adams.

The earliest American drawn and printed lithographs were two simple drawings of cottages in Pennsylvania executed in 1819 and 1820 by the artist Bass Otis.

VOLUNTEER

32.

Por que fue sensible.

He was closely followed and his technique improved upon by another painter, Rembrandt Peale, who was awarded the silver medal of the Franklin Institution in 1827 for his lithographed copy of his own oil portrait of Washington.

As in Europe, lithographic printers opened up print workshops which produced large editions of prints for the general public. **132** One of the most successful of these in the early days was Anthony Imbert, whose printing workshop opened in New York in 1825. Among his subsequent publications were a series of New York scenes by the architect A J Davis; *Niagara Falls* by Maraglia; and the series of Red Indian drawings by the famous Catlin.

Probably the best known print publishers in the States were Currier and Ives (Currier alone from 1836 to 1857; and Ives thereafter until 1901). They made many hundreds of series of popular prints – of the occurrences of the time, sporting prints, portraits and landscapes. Some of their most pleasant were the New York landscapes by Frances Farmer – notable are her print of a *Suburban Gothic Villa at Murray Hill;* and *Brooklyn from the United States Hotel, New York* drawn by the otherwise unknown E Whitefield in 1846.

As had the British in the 18th century, the Americans in the 19th used print-making as a political weapon and a means of making political commentary. The strong administration of General Jackson, combined with that gentleman's craggy appearance lent itself admirably to printmaking. There is the magnificent stipple engraving by J B Longacre after the oil portrait of General Jackson by Sully, and some clever political etchings by Edward Clay – especially a pair of 1831 '*Jackson Cleaning His Kitchen*' which refers to the 'Kitchen Cabinet', as a particularly obnoxious junta had come to be called; and '*Rats Leaving a Fallen House*'. In more serious vein, the same JB Longacre, who was later to become engraver to the US Mint published a portfolio of engravings and mezzotints – *The National Portrait Gallery of Distinquished Americans*.

With the transatlantic arrival of techniques similar to Baxter's, full chromolithography hit America with force. The first recorded series was printed by Max Rosenthal who set up his press in Philadelphia in 1849, and had the title *Wild Scenes and Wild Hunters*. Thereafter, as in Europe and especially in England, printmaking was as bad or as good as the artists who made the master drawings and the workmen who did the printing. The best artists naturally supervized their own prints, one of the most notable series being those by the painter Winslow Homer under the title *Campaign Sketches of the Civil War* printed and published by Perry of Boston, Massachusetts.

As in Europe, too, printmaking was used for purposes of fun. William Hamlin, a musical instrument maker and self-taught engraver made a reversible mezzotint which illustrated *The Splendours of Courtship and the Miseries of Marriage*. Coloured lithographs were used for theatre bills, book illustrations and music covers; and line engravings were the normal method of newspaper illustration, from which grew the American passion for comics.

Collecting Prints

The collector of prints has two immense advantages over his fellows in other fields of collecting – range of places where he may hope to discover additions to his collection, and range of prices. Because the print was the pre-camera version of, for example, the book illustration, the pin-up and the newspaper cartoon, and because it was natural for the 18th century bookseller to open up a print department for engravings, etchings and mezzotints, and later for chromolithographs and similar confections, one still finds many second-hand and

antiquarian bookshops with a stock of prints.

Then again, virtually every illustrated book before 1900 has prints of one kind or another as illustrations, in addition to the massive number of books *of* prints with commentary – for example those by Ackermann and Finden. Many of these books have now been taken to pieces and the prints sold individually; but it is always as well for a collector, should he buy such a volume cheaply, to collate it on the off-chance that it is complete, for the complete volume is infinitely more valuable and more desirable than the sum of its individual prints.

Beside bookshops, the print collector can hope to come across some additions to his collection in almost any junk or second-hand furniture shop, on the stalls in street markets, on the Paris quais, in specialist shops – military prints in military shops, sporting prints some-

times in sporting equipment shops, in the great auction rooms and in small auction sales anywhere in the world, in theatre and stage shops, as well, of course, in galleries specializing in prints and posters.

It is almost impossible to give any indication of price – a good example of Dürer's etching *The Landscape with the Cannon* sold recently at Sotheby's for £4,300 ($10,965) and Rembrandt's etching *Woman at the Bath with Hat beside her* at Christie's for 4,800 guineas ($12,348), whereas a friend of mine a few years ago bought the artist's proof of a George Stubbs' engraving for 5p. (13 cents). At each end of the scale, expertise is all. Choose the theme of your print collection, and then study the theme in as great depth as you have time for. Above all, enjoy it; for that's what collecting is all about, and prints are particularly attractive.

SCULPTURE & BRONZES

133 *15th century relief sculpture of the Baptism of Christ.*

134 *Late 15th century marble relief of Madonna and Child.*

Most of the greatest works by the world's famous sculptors are unobtainable by the private collector since they were created, and have remained, national monuments viewed in their giant form as part of the architectural framework of numerous capital cities. However, on a more intimate scale it is possible to acquire sculptural pieces that truly reflect the creative spirit of the final monument, and there is often an immense appeal in, say, a classical fragment or an 18th century terracotta maquette for a commemorative group. Such small-scale sculptures attract collectors principally for two reasons, firstly because they bear the marks of the original creative experiment of the sculptor, and secondly, because all sculpture embodies so expressively the individual style and spirit of the age in which it was created.

It is for this latter reason that in this short survey the field will be covered chronologically without separating the national characteristics of each period's sculpture.

Medieval and Gothic

The stylistic development from the Fall of Rome to the Renaissance is beautifully reflected in the highly collectable European ivories of those times, where the tense, angular style of the carving on caskets, statuettes and triptychs appeals directly to the emotions, irrespective of the basically religious content. The spirit is still there in late Gothic German woodcarving, exemplified in the 15th century relief sculpture of the Baptism of Christ. **133**

Renaissance

With the developments and discoveries of the

135 *Wooden relief by Grinling Gibbons 1648-1721.*

136 *School of Rubiliac bust of John Ray.*

period called the Renaissance, Italian artists revolutionized representational art. In the 15th century Italian marble relief of Madonna and Child attributed to Francesco di Simone Ferrucci, **134** the sense of real and physical emotions is conveyed in ways unknown to the *Gothic* sculptor. The precise achievements of the Renaissance are impossible to define in a short space, but this attractive group shows the concern for the development of sculpture in three dimensions and an understanding of human proportions.

Baroque

The Baroque style in sculpture appeared in its full glory in the monumental creations for the court of Louis XIV, and although many of these works were later reproduced as small bronze groups and statuettes, these do not really compare with the original. Far better to look for less grand works such as the wooden relief sculptures of Grinling Gibbons (1648-1721), where in this boxwood panel of *The Adoration of the Shepherds* **135** the baroque contrasts between light and dark are illustrated in the robustness of execution. The broad rhythmic control of forms, characteristic of the master sculptors Coysevox, Le Brun and Bernini, can also be seen in the less rare work of the German and Netherlandish 17th century carvers of ivory.

Rococo

After the strong and colourful expressions of the 17th century, the light, floating forms of the 18th century make a nice contrast. The work of Claudion (1738-1810) typifies perhaps best of all the imaginative freedom of

III

137

I.

138

139

141

142

the age, and the terracotta group of a Satyress with baby fauns **140** also has a lightness in execution which is a significant development from the baroque style. Certain groups in porcelain also have sculptural qualities, although they are not strictly sculpture. The same can be said for ormolu firedogs by eminent menuisiers such as Dubois or Caffieri.

English sculpture of the 18th century was dominated by foreign immigrants, notably François Roubiliac (1705-62) from France and Michael Rysbrack (1694-1770) from the Netherlands. The work of both these artists is extremely rare and expensive, but the stylistically similar work of their followers has considerable appeal, although clumsy compared with the work of the masters. This bust of John Ray **136** the naturalist, is copied contemporaneously from a Roubiliac bust executed in 1751 as one of the series of dons at Trinity College, Cambridge, and has attractive crisp, flowing lines.

But the field is wide and even an embossed picture by Samuel Dixon the mid-18th century Dubliner, would fit well into a sculptive collection. The photograph **137** of one of his famous Birds of Paradise series does not really convey the three dimensions found in these painted paper *basso-relievos*, the only rival to which are the smaller panels by Isaac Spackman, working in England. Filigree paper work comes under the same category of Works of Art, and although originating in ecclesiastical art of the 15th century, there was a great secular revival at the end of the 18th century.

Neo-Classical

The transition from the Rococo to the Neo-Classical

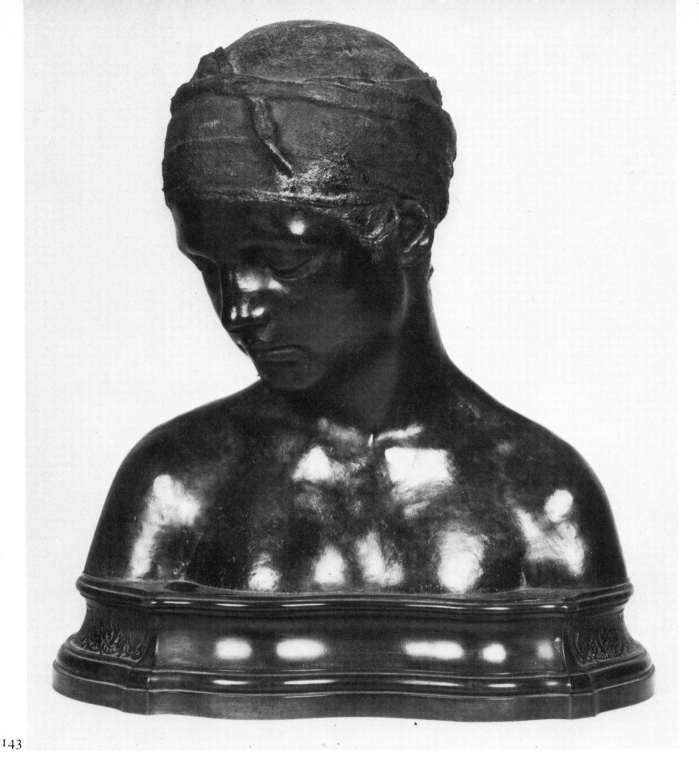

143

style which first began in France in the 1760s was a gradual process. Even in this unattributed marble bust, dated circa 1790 **139** the treatment of the hair and softness of expression still maintain some of the characteristics of the middle years of the century. However, in the Joseph Nollekins (1737-1823) portrait bust of Lady Elizabeth Monck **138**, there is the full tightness and control normally associated with the Neo-Classical style.

Some of the most sensitive work of the period is in small decorative bronzes, and this pair of gilt bronzes **141** has a calculated air of refined sensuality that epitomizes the stylistic transition between the Rococo and Neo-Classical styles. The sculptor of these was Falconet (1716-91) who specialized in the design of small-scale figures for use by the porcelain makers at Sèvres and by makers of decorative items such as clocks.

The Nineteenth Century

It is in the work of 19th century sculptors that collectors find their best opportunities of obtaining original pieces of individual interest.

Victorian Sculpture. Initially the dominating style was still the Neo-Classical, with the work of John Gibson (1790-1866) being outstanding. However the style of execution and conception gradually loosened to a far more individualistic *Romantic Style*, seen in the brooding terracotta of Thomas Carlyle **142** by Sir Edgar Boehm (1843-90), sculptor in ordinary to Queen Victoria. By the end of the century an interesting group of artists working in bronze grew up in London; the imaginative qualities of their work are shown in this restrained yet characterful bust of a girl **143** by Onslow Ford (1852-1901).

144 *Bronze by A. Carrier-Belleuse.*

145 *Turkish horse by Antoine Barye.*

French Nineteenth Century Sculpture. In certain respects, French sculptors have a more forcefully romantic approach than the English, and this can be clearly seen in the bronze figure of an infantryman by A Carrier-Belleuse (1824-97) who exhibited regularly in the Salons from 1861 onwards **143**.

Of particular significance is the French *Animalier School* of Sculptors headed by Antoine Barye (1796-1875) whose figure of a Turkish Horse **144** has superb rhythm and control, both in the general form and in the surface detailing. Not all the work of this school was on such a grand scale, as shown by the figure of a bear in a bath tub by Barye and a group of theatrical rats **146** by Alphonse Arson (1822-80).

However the leading French sculptor of the Romantic period is generally considered to be Jean-Baptiste Carpeau (1827-75) partly because of his immense success during his own lifetime; the terracotta bust, *La Rieuse aux Roses* **145** is a reasonable example of his small-scale work.

American Sculpture. During this period American sculptors came into their own and created numerous works of public and personal significance. In the former category the standing figure of Washington by John Quincy Adam Ward (1830-1910) expresses, in a modern idiom, all the dignity of period sculpture. In the other sector, Augustus Saint-Gandens (1848-1917) was a sculptor whose really inventive work was concentrated on small, impressionistic relief portraits of incomparable quality.

Many American sculptors trained in Europe, but returned home to develop their own personal styles. This is clearly seen in the animal sculpture of an artist such as SH Borghum (1868-1922) who studied under Fremiet in Paris but brought greater naturalistic freedom to his own work.

146 *La Rieuse aux Roses by Carpeau.*

147 *Animalier school: a theatrical rat by Alphonse Arson, a bear by Barye and an African elephant charging by Barye.*

148 *Tankard with enamel painting of the Four Evangelists, Bohemia, about 1610.*

149 *Late 19th century cameo vase with four figures, by Webb of Stourbridge.*

150 *Blue glass bowl circa 1810 from Bristol which had close links with the Irish glass trade. The bowl has a Greek key pattern in gold and is signed on the base I Jacobs Bristol. In 1806 Isaac Jacobs advertised himself as 'Glass manufactory to HM George 3.'*

151 *Carafe of ruby glass with opaque white overlay, cut and enamelled, Bohemia, about 1840.*

150

149

151

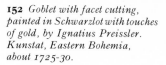

152 *Goblet with facet cutting, painted in Schwarzlot with touches of gold, by Ignatius Preissler. Kunstat, Eastern Bohemia, about 1725-30.*

under continuous re-heating, or by applied decoration to the finished glass specimen in the form of enamelling, gilding, cutting and engraving.

Glass in Antiquity

From the time of the early Christian era, ancient glassmakers applied almost all known processes of the craft, except the decorative treatment of acid etching.

By about 1500 BC hollow glass vessels had appeared in Egypt, produced by casting or pressing ground glass mixed to a paste into hollow moulds, or by hollowing out blocks of glass. Small colourful vessels, predominantly blue and yellow, were produced by the core technique, whereby a molten thread of glass was trailed around a pre-formed core. A great revival of this technique occurred in 700 and 600 BC and most of the surviving cored vessels available to the collector date from this period and were used largely for ointments and cosmetics. They are abundantly displayed in major museums, but the collector's rare chance comes only with a sale of antiquities, or at specialized dealers. Colourful mosaic and millefiori glass, made of composite glass canes, which were sliced, laid side by side and fused, were techniques known as early as 1500 BC, and were produced most prolifically from 323-330 BC until the third and fourth centuries AD.

Glassblowing is thought to have originated in or near Sidon about the year 1 AD and brought from there to Alexandria, which became a flourishing glass centre. From that moment onward, glass making became a craft of limitless possibilities. The very first blown objects are probably the small club-shaped *tearbottles*, frequent funerary finds supposedly for holding the mourners' tears. They often shown an attractive iridescence, a type of weathering due to long exposure to damp earth or air, and make desirable collectors' items since they may still be found at a reasonable cost of just a few pounds. Small mould blown relief glasses are associated with second and third century Sidon, and hellenistic-inspired mould-blown cups and beakers with inscriptions and names of the craftsmen were produced by a group of glassblowers led by one Ennion, whose pupils established workshops in a wide area from North Africa to Gaul. Glass broke away from the confines of luxury ware and emerged as a material for domestic use. The glassmakers, travelling across Europe in the wake of the Roman legions, adapted their techniques to satisfy requirements for glassbottles and storage containers of practical use.

Nevertheless, artistic glassware was still made in the Mediterranean areas. Greece and Italy produced excellent cameo work, and this art was ably applied to the media of glass. The notorious Portland (or Barberini) Vase in the British Museum dating from the first century AD is one of the finest examples of early cameo glass.

The *Fondi d'Oro* technique was popular during the first four or five centuries AD. Here goldleaf is applied in the form of etched designs and sandwiched between

The basic ingredients of glass are silica sand, a fluxing agent such as soda ash, and limestone which serves as a stablizer. Lead crystal has a composition of silica sand of the whitest, iron-free quality, potash and lead oxide. Fusion takes place at a temperature of about 1500° centigrade, and when cooled to 800° centigrade the glass mass, that is the *metal*, will be workable and under given conditions remain so for about twenty to thirty minutes. Addition of cullet *(scrap glass)* to the batch will assist melting, and introduction of various mineral oxides determines the quality, the hardness of the metal, its refractive property, colour and transparency.

Glass can be moulded, blown, drawn, cast and pressed. Decorative effects may be achieved either by manipulating the ductile glass mass into all manner of shapes

153 *Goblet and cover, clear colourless glass with enamelled and gilt decoration. Venetian, late 15th century.*

154 *Venetian Goblet in latticinio glass. Late 17th or early 18th century.*

two transparent glass layers. Because of the decorative symbols employed, *Fondi d'Oro* is frequently referred to as early Christian or Jewish gold sandwich glass, though this does not necessarily imply the faith of the glassmakers involved.

The greatest triumph of the glassmakers art was achieved in the *vasa diatreta* – the cage cup, (100-300 AD) produced by undercutting the outer part of the wall to form a network which remains attached by a few struts. The frieze around the upper half of the cup is carved to form the Greek or Latin inscription. Though most existing specimens have been discovered in the Rhine area, the effect is strikingly reminiscent of eastern ivory carving, and one might suspect some oriental inspiration.

A flourishing glass industry had been established in Byzantium long before the disintegration of the Roman Empire. Craftsmen worked under most favourable conditions, and the adoption of Christianity inspired building on a grand scale; mosaics made up of thousands of coloured glass cubes (tesserae) blazed from the splendidly proportioned walls and domes of the Byzantine Basilica.

Islamic Glass

In 634 AD, the Byzantine army was wiped out by Muslim forces, and with the rise of Islam a distinct Islamic style emerged also in artistic glassmaking.

Glass produced during the period of Roman domination is often loosely referred to as *Roman glass*, although it may well have been the work of a Syrian gaffer (master blower). The description *Islamic glass* usually refers to specimens decorated by enamelling and gilding, and produced during the Islamic period; how-

155 *American 1835. New England Glass Company, blown apple paper weight. The apple rests on a cushion of clear crystal glass.*

156 *Left to right, top row: Clichy garland weight with nine white and green roses; Baccarat pansy weight with deep wine-red petals above three smaller yellow and mauve petals centred on a whorl and stardust cluster; Baccarat close millefiore weight inscribed 'B 1848' with several silhouettes; Baccarat patterned weight with alternative blue and white florettes, each one centred by a whorl and stardust cluster*

florette. Middle row: Clichy turquoise swirl weight centred on green and pink set-up; Clichy miniature faceted weight, the inner circle consisting of nine pink and green roses; miniature Clichy weight centred upon a fine white and pink Clichy rose; Clichy swirl weight with alternate lime green and white threads. Bottom row: Clichy scattered millefiore weight set in clear glass; extremely rare Baccarat thousand petal rose with star cut base; extremely rare St Louis four-coloured crown weight, consisting of blue and yellow, red and green alternating with white latticinio; Clichy chequer weight with a

155

156

central pink and green rose, the two circles of canes divided by latticinio.

157 Three lacy pressed glass pieces: (L-R) Sugar bowl with cover, probably Providence Flint Glass Works, 1831-3, or possibly Boston and Sandwich, circa 1830-40. Lamp, New England Glass Company, circa 1830.

158 Lamp by G Argy-Rousseau and A Bourraine. Made in France of pâte-de-cristal at the end of the 19th century.

157

158

159 *1. Wine glass with funnel bowl on a colour twist stem and high conical foot.*
2. One of a pair of rare opaque twist wine glasses. The bucket bowls are set on a double series of opaque twist stems, on high conical folded feet.

3. Large wine glass with deep double ogee bowl, and a multiple air twist stem with central swollen knop on a plain conical foot.

4. Fine baluster wine glass with short funnel bowl solid at the base with a tear, a stem consisting of a short plain section, a large triple annular knop above a plain section and a base knop on a domed and folded foot.

5. Light baluster wine glass, with trumpet bowl.

ever the craftsman could have been Mesopotamian, Persian or Egyptian, and the work embellished in a variety of techniques.

The finest achievement of Islamic glass art is the enamelling and gilding produced between 1250 and 1400 AD at the main glass centres of Raqqa, Aleppo, and Damascus. There is very little chance here for the private collector who must be wary of forgery, but the superb craftsmanship may be admired particularly in the rare 14th century mosque lamps displayed in major museums.

The Slump in the West

Frankish and Seine-Rhine glasshouses were now attempting to produce glassware without the guidance of Roman-imported know-how. In due course, a liquid-greenish metal became typical for the European forest glasshouses, and this *Waldglas* (Forest glass) was still made long after the rediscovery of decolourizing with manganese dioxide (glassmaker's soap). Fragments of Roman and Forest glass come to light quite frequently outside archeological sites, and with such finds an informative collection may be built up.

Window Glass

This essential industry did not succumb to economic or political pressure, and window glass was produced by two methods – the *broadsheet* and the *crown* technique. By the first, the gaffer blew an elongated bubble (the paraison), which is cut off at both ends, resulting in a glass cylinder which is split lengthwise and flattened. The crown technique entailed cutting off the paraison from the blowpipe and transferring it to an iron rod, the pontil. This was then freely rotated in front of the furnace

opening and frequently reheated. By thus applying centrifugal force, the opened bubble spread, resulting in a large circular pane of glass with the thickened *bull's eye* in the centre.

Stained Glass

The earliest colour stain (15th century) was the yellow obtained by coating the glass pane with silver nitrate and subsequent annealing. Overpainting was carried out with *Schwarzlot*, a low viscosity mixture prepared from copper oxide. Coloured glass was prepared from a coloured batch. By the 17th century the stained glass window began to disappear, though a charming *small-art* developed, particularly in Switzerland, of small stained, painted and engraved glass panels. This is a collectors' field which has as yet not been over-exploited. Purchase, and price, is a matter of luck, depending greatly on the knowledge of buyer, and seller.

Many later artists applied staining, Schwarzlot and transparent enamelling techniques to hollow glass ware: Johann Schaper (1621-70) in Nürnberg, Ignaz Preissler (c 1675-1733) **152** and son working in Bohemia, Samuel Mohn (1762-1815) of Dresden, and the son Gottlob Samuel (1789-1825) who moved to Vienna, where he greatly influenced another skilful artist working in transparent enamelling techniques, Anton Kothgasser (1769-1851). **148** Vessels decorated by transparent enamelling, particularly the work of early 19th century artists, appear regularly at good auction sales, but tend to be expensive. **151**

Venice

To prevent further fire hazard to the city, the Venetian glass industry was moved to the island of Murano

160 *Bowl with gilt rim and painted in delicate enamel colours with arms, foliage and a group of trophies, and trellis patterns within rococo shell cartouche.*

161 *Globular bottles of the early 18th century; (a) sealed E F 1702, (b) the later, taller shape which evolved, a bottle sealed S Holloway 1726, (c) a squarer mallet shaped bottle with a later silver mount added.*

161

in 1291, still the centre of Italian glassmaking today. The 15th century brought a revival of ancient techniques in millefiori, mosaic and marbled glass. Gilding and enamelling in brilliant dots and scale motifs is typical for this period, and enamelled figural representations found on deep blue or green goblets is associated in particular with the Berovieri family of glassmakers. **153** The Venetian development of *cristallo*, a clear, fluid, soda-fluxed glass metal which cooled quickly and required great dexterity, revolutionized the entire concept of glassmaking. Due to the re-discovery of decolourizing, cristallo was almost colourless, provided it was blown thin enough. It was therefore unsuitable for refiring, an essential for durable enamelling, but its fluidity seduced the gaffer to use all manner of fantastic shapes with trailed, applied and pincered decoration, often in a typical shade of blue glass. The serpentine or winged glass was representative of this mood and became most elaborate by the 17th century.

Though Murano glassworkers were under strict surveillance and heavily punished if caught, many did escape abroad, as did also the craftsmen from Altare near Genoa, who were not subjected to such restrictions. Glass *à la façon de Venise* had become fashionable and the European courts were eager to employ Italian glass makers.

The lace-like effect of *latticinio* glass was achieved by embedding white glass canes in a clear glass matrix which was then manipulated in intricate patters **154**. Shallow diamond engraving appears on cristallo glass during the 16th century, particularly on specimens made in England, Tyrol and Holland. **173**

With the establishment of Venetian inspired work-shops in all important European glass centres, the *Waldglas industry* receded in importance. Remnants of medieval domestic glassware gave way to more sophisticated vessels. The *Passglas* with applied zone rings, the tall *Stangenglas* and the large *Humpen* appeared as the most popular drinking vessels. Gay, enamelled decoration showed motifs of great variety – commemorative, historical, regional, domestic and heraldic – and was popular particularly in Bohomia and Germany. Finely enamelled Humpen will be priced at several hundred pounds, and more. Nineteenth century reproductions, which are plentiful, should not deceive the experienced collector. The modern glass will show a uniform greenish colour and the high kick in the base will most likely be absent. An important derivation from medieval forms, the *Roemer*, remained popular in the Lowlands and Germany well into the 18th century. It is a large goblet of deliberate greenish tint, with a hollow, spreading foot made of spirally wound glass and an ovoid bowl. The stem is decorated by applied raspberry prunts.

The Netherlands

The glass produced at the centres of Antwerp and Liège with the help of Italian know-how and workmanship is almost indistinguishable from the Venetian home product, and included latticinio and *ice* (crackle or frosted) glass of very good quality. Fine early glass *à la façon de Venise* is often Museum material and may be priced accordingly. A somewhat colourful revival took place during the later 19th century on the Continent, and in England. Much of it is of excellent quality and should not be scoffed at.

The finest contribution to glass art, however, was made by 17th and 18th century Netherland engravers who had sophisticated techniques and a highly original approach. Calligraphic engraving in the form of cursory script was applied to substantial drinking glasses such as the Roemer but is also found on wine-flasks of the mid- and later 17th century. Some of the most able artists in this field were women – Anna Roemers Visscher (1583-1651) and her sister, with the Jacobsz brothers of Leyden and William Heemskerk, were the best known engravers in this technique. The peak of artistic achievement was attained in the stippling technique, whereby the desired motifs are engraved by means of minute dots applied with the diamond point or steel needle. The finest stipple engraving is attributed to David Wolff (1732-98). Existing specimens are all dated between the years 1784-96, and the delightful putti and exquisitely dressed children typify rococo charm. Stippled

162
163

164

165

glasses are relatively rare and will fetch very large sums at auction.

By about 1725 the Italian-established Dagnia glasshouse at Newcastle had developed a glassmetal of the most brilliant, clear, white quality, which was in great demand by Netherland artists. It is not surprising therefore, that the finest Dutch engraving is found on the finest English glass.

British Isles

Glaziers from Normandy and the Lorraine came to the British shores from the 7th century onward and were chiefly employed in supplying window and stained glass.

In 1567, Jean Carré, a Lorrainer, was granted a licence for making window glass and obtained a patent to manufacture glass *à la façon de Venise*. For this purpose he engaged a Venetian, Giacomo (Jacopo) Verzelini (1522-1606), and about nine glasses exist which can to this day be definitely attributed to Verzelini's Crutched Friars glasshouse. They show the typical Italian characteristics of the hollow- (often mould-) blown knop of the stem and the folded foot, a method of doubling under the rim at the edge to strengthen the glassmetal. The glasses are of ample proportion, with diamond point engraving in the hatched, Italian fashion attributed to a Frenchman, Anthony de Lisle. Occasionally there is gilding, and more rarely enamelled decoration. The metal is of a soft, faintly greenish tint.

With wood becoming scarce, the 1615 *Proclamation touching glasses* forbade the use of woodfuel, an act which encouraged the coal-mining industry.

In 1676 George Ravenscroft (1618-81), a protégé of the Worshipful Company of Glass Sellers in London, succeeded in developing his 'perticuler sort of Christaline Glasse resembling rock Chrystall,' and from 1677 his best specimens are marked with the Ravens Head seal, though crizzling, a defect due to excessive alkali content, was not entirely eliminated for some years.

Ravenscroft's success was obtained by the addition of lead oxide to the batch, and his heavy glassmetal has a unique watery limpidity and clarity of colour without the brittle hardness of Venetian cristallo, and excellent refractive properties. Fusing at lower temperature than cristallo, it remains workable for a longer period.

The 18th century drinking glass is a desirable as well as a precious possession. Styles are so varied that glasses are grouped and dated according to the features incorporated in bowl and foot design. **159** The Venetian inspired baluster stem is one of the most important characteristics in English glasses between the years 1682-1730, and of Venetian inspiration too is the development of the enamel and colour twist stem, a most attractive technique practised from about 1745-80. Intricate combined twists or rare colours in colour-twist stems will enhance both beauty and value of the glass. The stem with enclosed airtwist was probably developed from the accidentally and later purposely introduced air bubble – or tear – and represents one of the most

admirable and beautiful facets of glassmaking, appearing first in trumpet bowl, drawn stem glasses about 1730.

The most elegant product of the English glasshouse is the Newcastle Baluster, a tall glass with a bell or funnel bowl, and, generally, a plain foot. Knopped stems often include tears and airtwists and bowls may show excellent engraving by Dutch artists.

Commemorative glasses of all kinds were popular during the 18th century. A special group is represented by the Jacobite glasses, recalling the rebellions of 1715 and 1745 with engraving of Jacobite symbols. The proportion of the drinking glass is an important guide for the collector. In the English specimen the circumference of the foot about equals that of the rim of the bowl, and the foot should rise at the centre to meet the stem.

English rococo is represented in the enamelled decoration seen best in opaque white glass produced mainly in the Bristol and Staffordshire areas. Michael Edkins (1733-1811) and James Giles (1713-1780), though differing in style, belong to the elite of 18th century

129

enamellers and gilders decorating glass and china ware. In Newcastle, William Beilby (1740-1819) and his sister Mary (1749-97) produced exquisite work in white and coloured enamels, and the Jacobs family at Bristol fine gilding on Bristol blue table glass. **150**

After the doubling of the glass tax in 1777, some of the best cutters emigrated to Ireland which was granted full freedom of trade in 1779. English-supported glasshouses sprang up in Waterford, Cork, Belfast and Dublin, producing heavy quality cut tableglass, and from 1780-1825 we may speak of an Anglo-Irish period. Slight engraving found on Irish glass is generally not up to the standard of its fine cutting. A more light-hearted effect was achieved in Nailsea (new Bristol) glass with coloured or opaque white loops and bands, and speckled bottle glass. With the 18th century begins the real collectors' period. The great variety in glass design permits selection to suit most tastes and means. Rare twists, Jacobite glasses and specimens decorated by known artists will be accordingly expensive, but Bristol wines in the typical blue and emerald green as well as decanters, without embellishment, will make a rewarding collection, and glass objects in Nailsea style will delight the collector without straining his pocket.

In the later 19th century, the finest work was produced in the Stourbridge area where John Northwood (1836-1902) and the Woodall Brothers initiated the artistic revival of cameo glass techniques, and Thomas Webb's Company attracted many excellent Bohemian glass cutters. **149** Webb's cameo glass will appear at most specialized art nouveau sales and like fine specimens by Gallé and his contemporaries has rocketed in price beyond all proportion. However, smaller objects such

as scent bottles can still be purchased without necessarily going into three-figure sums. Early sealed bottles are desirable, available, but rising in price. **161**

Bohemia

Caspar Lehman (1570-1622), lapidary to Rudolf II at Praque, is credited to have been the first to apply wheel engraving to the brittleness of baroque soda glass. By the late 17th century, a more suitable glassmetal had been developed, and during the early 18th century an unrivalled technique in Hoch- and Tiefschnitt akin to rock crystal cutting – high and low relief cutting had been evolved by Bohemian and Silesian glass artists. With commercial expansion, the influence of Bohemian glass art became world wide. A group of 18th century glasses show a revival of gold sandwich glass, and the Austrian, Mildner (1763-1808) developed a very individual variation in the form of inserted medallions. Johann Kunckel (1630-1703) developed his gold-ruby glass at Potsdam and by the early 19th century Bohemia had established herself as leader in the field of coloured glass. The most original work was produced at the workshops of Bedrich Egerman (1777-1864). **167, 169** He revived techniques of stained and marbled glass, particularly the *Lythialin stone* glass which was produced not only in the well known red, but also in other colour modulations. A black opaque glass was developed in the South Bohemian factory of Count Buquoy – the *Hyalith* glass, which was usually embellished by cutting and gilding. In North Bohemia, Josef Riedel produced a fluorescent glass, greenish or yellowish in colour – the *Annagrün* and *Annagelb*. Attractively coloured, cut and engraved overlay glass became a Bohemian speciality and was exported – and imitated – all over the world. Good 19th century Bohemian glass frequently appears at sales and may be bought from shops and dealers. Egerman's Lythialin, and glass produced by known glasshouses and artists can be expensive, but there is still plenty of scope. Spa glasses of the Biedermeier period in red and amber overlay will make an attractive collection, nor should scent bottles nor milk glass be neglected.

France

France's great contribution to medieval glass art was in the development of window and stained glass techniques. In the later 17th century, an enterprising and avant-garde glassmaker of Orlèans, Bernard Perrot, produced mouldblown beakers and scent bottles which are delightful examples of this early period. However, the most avidly collected and collectable French glass was produced during the 19th century. Baccarat created a brilliant glassmetal in fine colours, including uranium (fluorescent) glass, enriched by excellent cutting. During 1823-48, the ingenious experiments of George Bontemps at Choisy-le-Roi in reviving latticinio and millefiori techniques, were instrumental in the creation of the French paperweight.

The three main factories producing this colourful extravaganza were Baccarat, St Louis and Clichy, and some specimens are marked with dates and initials. Millefiori and flower-weights were made by all factories.

166 *Cut celery vase, gift of the Bakewells to Henry Clay Fry when he opened his glass factory in Pittsburgh about 1867. Pittsburgh, Bakewell, Page and Bakewell c 1825.*

167 *Lithyalin flaçon by Egermann, cut and gilded circa 1820.*

168 *Webb cameo glass vase.*

167

St Louis is perhaps the least conventional with reptile weights and often a characteristically flattened dome. Clichy favours a swirl pattern, Baccarat specializes in sulphides – enclosing medallions or such like of metallic or refractory material. This process (cristallo-ceramie) was ably exploited in England by Apsley Pellat. A star-cut base is a further Baccarat characteristic. **156**

With the foundation of the École de Nancy, Emile Gallé (1846-1904) created a new art concept, particularly in glassmaking techniques. Emphasis was on individual studio work of great originality based on the fullest exploitation of the glass metal. The influence of Gallé's cameo-glass technique was enormous. Among the best exponents of the École de Nancy were the Daum brothers at Nancy and Muller Frères of Lunéville. Brocard specialized in Islamic style enamelling, Cros, Dammouse, Décorchemont, Argy-Rousseau and Walter produced most interesting specimens in *pâte de verre*. With the work of René Lalique (1860-1945), which ranged from exquisite jewellery in glowing enamels to architectural fountains, and the powerful glass forms of Marinot (1882-1960), France has arrived at the summit of modern glass art.

The veritable boom in the field of 19th century paperweights and the extravagant prices fetched by quality art nouveau glass and studio work will dismay the aspiring collector. He should not ignore the charming glass specimens in opaline of soft pastel shade with fine gilding and enamelling. There is no problem regarding availability and prices are favourable.

168

169 *Left to right, top: Cut overlay perfume bottle in the shape of a boot, Bohemian, early 19th century; flat lithyalin glass bottle by F. Egermann or imitator; cut and highly polished lithyalin glass bottle by Egermann with ground glass stopper and silver plated screw cap, both circa 1830: waisted perfume bottle in clear glass cut on the wheel, with gold mount set with stones and ground glass stopper under hinged cap, possibly French, early 19th century.*
Centre: Cologne or smelling bottle in cameo glass with opaque white cherry motif on light blue background and ground glass stopper

and hinged silver lid, made by Thomas Webb and Sons, circa 1887; acorn shaped perfume flask, English, early 19th century. Bottom: Two glass scent bottles in cloisonné gilt cases, glass probably English, metalwork Chinese, both late 18th century.

America

The earliest glassmaking attempts were probably made by English settlers in Jamestown, Virginia in 1608, and again in 1621. These ventures failed, and it was not until the 18th century that a glass industry became established on a successful scale.

In 1739 Caspar Wistar (1696-1752), a German-born brass-button manufacturer, established his glasshouse some thirty miles south-east of Philadelphia, appropriately naming the spot Wistarberg. Although the main output consisted of windowglass and bottles, tableware in the form of brown, amber, green, blue and turquoise vessels with wave patterns, applied threads and prunts, became characteristic of Wistarberg glass. Craftsmen from Germany and Holland joined the factory, which closed down in 1780. Under Wistarberg influence, a free-blown glass style of pleasing, bold form emerged, known as the South Jersey style. South Jersey glass was produced in attractive, clear colours, with amber, green and aquamarine being the most popular. A distinctive theme was expressed by the lily-pad motif, an applied glass decoration surrounding the lower half of the vessel.

163 The South Jersey tradition was kept alive by the craftsmen of the New York State glasshouses during the second quarter of the 19th century, until about 1860.

Henry William Stiegel (1729-1785), an ironsmith by trade, established his first glasshouse at Elizabeth Furnace in 1763, and by 1769 was owner of three factories in Pennsylvania. Glassworkers were imported from Germany and England, and tableware of good flint glass shows decorative enamelling in a rustic, continental style, well suited to the taste of a German community. Mould-blown glass in colour with a preference for amethyst and a recurrence of the daisy in a diamond motif is associated with Stiegel-type glass.

Among these influential personalities, John Frederick Amelung (1741-1798) was the only one who arrived on the American glassmaking scene as an experienced glassmaker. When he came to the colonies in 1784, he was accompanied by sixty-eight practical glassworkers engaged from various parts of Germany and Bohemia. By February 1785 he had established his New Bremen Glass Manufactory near Frederick, Maryland.

Existing presentation goblets and flasks in fine quality glass show expert craftsmanship and competent engraving in the Continental manner. Excavated fragments indicate that Amelung also produced pattern-moulded glass in various colours and that experiments were made with a lead glass composition. Amelung's

glass is probably the most sophisticated product of the 18th-century American glass industry, and it was unfortunate that due to over-ambitious expansion and financial losses suffered at the burning down of the glass house in 1790, the factory was forced to cease operation after only eleven years.

One of the first glasshouses to produce cut and engraved tableware in English and Continental style was the Pittsburgh Flint Glass Manufactory founded in 1808 by Benjamin Bakewell and Edward Ensell, an Englishman. **166** Bakewell's glasshouse produced lead glass of extremely fine quality and in 1817 made a superb table service ordered by President Munroe.

In 1818 the New England Glass Company was formed by a group of Boston business men who had purchased the defunct Boston Porcelain and Glass Company. One of the partners, Deming Jarves (1790-1869) established his own factory at Sandwich, which was incorporated in 1826 as the Boston and Sandwich Glass Company. After Jarves perfected his practical glass pressing machine, the technique spread rapidly and revolutionized the industry throughout the world. **162**

Early American pressed ware was usually of fine quality lead glass, and by 1825 a new style in glass design had been developed, the so-called *Lacy*, produced by small dots in the mould. The stipple-pattern of Lacy glass has the appearance of textile or embroidery, and serves as a background to the great variety of popular motifs and designs. **157** The best known objects in Lacy glass are the small cup-plates impressed with emblems, often of commemorative nature, and delightful salt cellars – small troughs designed in the French Empire or Rococo style, in clear colourless or coloured glass. An

170 *Tiffany Poppy Lamp* **171** *Blown and pressed and cut oil lamp, possibly Midwest, Pittsburgh area, c 1835-40.*

170   171

interesting collector's field is provided by mould-blown or pressed pictorial and historical pocket flasks, popular from about 1780, and made in several colours.

Craftsmen from French glasshouses such as Baccarat and St Louis were engaged by American companies and about the mid-19th century paperweights were produced in a number of techniques. The most original achievements are attractive, single fruit paperweights of blown glass in naturalistic colours and near life-size.
155 Produced by the New England Glass Company between 1853 and 1880, they are probably the work or inspiration of a former Baccarat craftsman, Francois Pierre. Apparently they have no identical counterpart in Continental glass design.

The Art Nouveau movement brought overwhelming response particularly in the work of Louis Comfort Tiffany (1848-1933). The company was established in 1878 and a number of unusually interesting glass techniques were developed due to experiments with metallic films and inclusions. The most successful of Tiffany's achievements is the 'Favrile', an iridescent glass in brilliant peacock colours. The influence of this concept is particularly pronounced in the Papillon glass made by Lötz Witwe at Klostermühle, Bohemia.

In 1864, a cheaper substitute for lead glass – the lime-soda glass developed by William Leighton of the Wheeling Glass Factory in West Virginia – spelled disaster for some of the manufacturers of fine quality lead glass and they were forced to close down.

The New England Glass Company ceased operations in 1888, and the manager, Edward D Libbey, acquired the Charter and moved the company to Toledo, Ohio, where fine glass is made to this day. The Corning

172

glassworks, reorganized in 1875 from an amalgamation of earlier factories, are now incorporated in the Steuben Glass Company who produce high quality crystal glass.

Understandably, little early American glass appears on the European market. Tiffany, with established overseas branches, is well represented, and in line with French art nouveau studio work, prices are extremely high.

China

Chinese glass is substantially thick, of smooth texture, and slightly oily to the touch. Edges are usually ground smooth. Although it appears that glassmaking techniques were known in China during antiquity, the finest work was produced during the 18th century, and this is marvellously exploited in the Chinese – and Japanese – snuffbottles of the period, notably between 1735-95 (Ch'ien Lung). Regarded more as a means of applying skilful techniques than as an artistic material in itself, Chinese glass treatment displays exquisite *tours de force* seen in the medicine and snuffbottles painted delicately from the inside, and the tiny carved animal forms in the jewel-like colours of Peking or Mandarin glass. The Oriental influence in Europe art forms initiated the 18th-century chinoiserie movement, and during the later 19th century a renewed interest is reflected by the Japonism found in Art Nouveau. It was from a visit to the Snuffbottle Collection at the South Kensington (now Victoria and Albert) Museum, London, that Gallé conceived his inspiration for cameo glass techniques. Fine Chinese glass, apart from scent bottles, is rare. Scent and snuffbottles are very much collected and prices are still within reasonable limits.

Spain

Due to geographical location and the course of historical events, Spanish glass development was influenced by both East and West. Rustic glass in fanciful shapes with applied decoration was a reminder of Syrian techniques, and during the 16th and early 17th centuries Islamic and Venetian artisans inspired attractive enamelling with *latticinio* techniques still popular during the 18th century. The *Almorrata* (a sprinkler), the *Càntir* (for holding water, resembling a footed teapot), the *Porró* (a long-spouted wine carafe), oil lamps and wall fonts are domestic vessels produced in quantity. The Royal Factory of La Granja de San Ildefonso was established in 1728, and experienced European glassworkers were engaged for this enterprise. The best decorative techniques are seen in engraved and gilded glass with predominantly floral motifs which are also a popular design in colourful enamelled work. Spanish glass may not always be appreciated or recognized as such by the average collector, and consequently prices are fairly low, except for the very early enamelled ware and the *façon de Venise* specimens.

Russia

Whilst European art flourished under the influence of the Renaissance movement, Russian cultural and artistic life lay confined under Mongol domination. Not until the mid-17th century were some glasshouses set up with the assistance of Swedish and Italian craftsmen. Glass was produced mainly for the Imperial Court, and by the early 18th century Peter the Great had established his glasshouse on Sparrow Hill. It was subsequently moved nearer to the new capital, St Petersburg. Two privately owned glassworks belonging to the Malt'sov and Bakhmet'yev families also branched out with good table glass. Bakhmet'yev, a talented glassmaker, produced fine luxury ware with good enamelling, gilding and cutting, as well as coloured and milk glass, very much on the lines of crystal glass produced by France and Bohemia. Between 1753 and 1765, Professor Lomonosov, though failing to produce glass *à la façon de Venise* as required by the Court, created some fine work in his favourite medium, the mosaic picture on a grand scale. A more individual and colourful glass style is shown in some of the pieces made at the Bakhmet'yev and St Petersburg factories during the later 19th century. Their designs show a revival of Russian folk motifs fused with the great heritage of Byzantium, and some coloured speciments are stained, enamelled or gilded. There is enormous potential in all fields of 19th century Russian art and this is very much reflected in today's prices. Eighteenth century wine glasses with engraving are obtainable at reasonable cost, but really fine 19th century art glass is rare.

Scandinavia

In Scandinavia, glassmaking followed a conservative course with at first Venetian-inspired thin blown vessels which became more robust to suit the cutting and

 173

engraving techniques of German immigrant craftsmen. Much of the glass was made for the Royal household and by the late 17th and early 18th century fine chandeliers and table glass based on English design and techniques testify to excellent craftsmanship. The factories of Kungsholm and Nestetangen were eager to improve their products with the help of foreign know-how. During the 18th century, glassblowers from Newcastle and engravers from Germany, such as Heinrich Gottlieb Köhler and Villas Vinter, joined the industry. Today some of the finest glass is produced at factories which are descendants from these 18th-century glassworks, with Ørrefors and Kosta in Sweden, Hadeland and the Norsk Glassverk at Mangor in Norway, representing modern glass art at its best. Attractive plain decanters may be found occasionally at reasonable cost.

174

175 *A pair of English 16th century gloves presented to his friend and counsellor Sir Anthony Denny by Henry VIII. They are embroidered in red silk with gold and silver lace.*

176 *A late 18th century tea-caddy, made in India for the English market; veneered in ivory and engraved with English houses.*

Needlework

There is an enormous amount of needlework of many different kinds and descriptions which has come down to us and which makes fascinating collecting.

Stumpwork is characteristic of the embroidery of the 17th century, both in Europe and America. The Metropolitan Museum of Art in New York has a charming mirror, set in a border of embroidered birds and figures and in its original tortoiseshell frame. There is also a basket of beadwork, stump-work and wire, typical of the late 17th century. The Great Exhibition of 1851 in England showed beautiful examples of Continental hand embroidery. For instance, Switzerland offered needlework, embroidered pictures, worked handkerchiefs and sewed muslins. From France came tatting or *frivolité*, which is a sort of knotted lace work; and, from Ireland, crochet work.

At the beginning of the 18th century, women occupied themselves making decorative panels for the walls, usually floral designs, and later small exquisite pictures of flowers and other subjects worked on either silk, twill, sarsenet, or paper. Typical flowers of this period were striped tulips, lilies, forget-me-nots, carnations, moss-roses and auriculas.

The commercial needlework patterns began about 1804, the brain-child of one Phillipson. Frau Witch of Berlin perfected the idea, and by 1830 the craze for Berlin wool work was in full swing. The Victorian product, highlighted with beads from about 1850, presents rather a garish contrast to the elegant Georgian work. The early biblical themes and romantic troubadour style, the portraits of the British Royal Family, and of animals on cushions, chair backs, footstools and smoking caps are still easily found. The exotic birds were often worked in *plush stitch*, when the cutting of the loops gave an effect which resembled a thick carpet. Other work was patchwork, a favourite occupation in America also. Firescreens were also a popular needlework subject for decoration.

Boxes for needlework

Victorian work boxes and wooden boxes are not hard to find and may be made of rosewood, walnut, Turnbridge-ware (which brought fame to Turnbridge Wells in Kent in the early 19th century), satinwood, Chinese lacquer and tortoiseshell. Ivory boxes might come from the Far East, but it is a Western creation to divide the workbox into small compartments and trays. The linings of the workboxes are coloured and sometimes quilted or padded, and some Regency boxes are made of tooled leather with a miniature needle-case in replica inside. Tunbridge-ware wood mosaic boxes are made in the fascinating veneering technique of gluing different coloured strips of wood on to a base, in geometric chequerboard, floral or picture patterns. This intricate work was imitated to a limited extent in America, both by amateur and professionals, who produced inlaid tables and other objects.

Although the boxes are comparatively easy to find, their fittings are quite another matter. These might include steel scissors, a Tunbridge-ware case for silks; ivory, wood or mother-of-pearl discs, shaped like snowflakes and meant for silk or cotton holders; pins and needles; thread-waxers; bodkin-cases of beadwork or carved ivory; a tambour hook for making a chain, stiletto-shaped sometimes like an animal or person.

177 *Bisque. Fully dressed doll by Armand Marselle. Circa 1910*

178 *A mid-19th century toy butcher's shop. This is not a model, like the far larger ones to be seen in the Bethnal Green Museum, but a child's plaything.*

One made of wood is probably a Napoleonic prisoner-of-war relic, shaped like Bonaparte himself. Pincushions, of all shapes and sizes may be there, sewing-clamps or steel clamps fitted with pin cushions, bobbin-holders, and needlecases in great variety. The clamps were to help with pinning up the hems on tablecloths and sheets before the invaluable sewing-machine was invented.

Thimbles and Chatelaines

Roman metal thimbles were the same shape as ours today, but in their earliest form thimbles used to be made from bone or wood and were simply tied on to the finger as a kind of shield. Examples of thimbles from the 12th and 13th centuries can be seen in museums in America and Europe, but pride of place goes to an early Egyptian *needle-pusher*, made of stone, and believed to date back to 2,000 BC.

Collectable thimbles can be found from about 1700, made of silver and different coloured gold, engraved and set with precious stones. Thimbles may also be made of porcelain, mother-of-pearl, brass, steel, copper, and ivory.

In the 18th century thimbles came under the general heading of *toys*. The glass thimbles come from Bohemia and Venice, the wooden ones from Germany and Austria, the porcelain and metal ones from England as well as the Continent. They were all much in demand when women expected to spend a great deal of time in sewing. Moreover, these valuable little treasures often has special cases of leather, ivory, wood, shagreen and tortoiseshell. An American invention was the thimble-hand, made of glass, with the fingers arranged to carry thimbles. Wooden acorns, walnuts and eggs of various kinds often housed thimbles, and later some of the most luxurious ones were contained in cases made by Fabergé's craftsmen.

The chatelaine was a large metal hook, sometimes gold or silver, sometimes steel, which fastened on to the belt. On it there hung by chains such necessities of the housewife as scissors, a thimble in a bucket, keys, a notebook, a needlecase, a pencil or other objects in everyday use. From about 1800 to 1840 chatelaines were out of favour on account of the fashions of the period, but many interesting Victorian ones are to be found. The various objects attached to chatelaines are by no means always the originals, however. The American version usually only accommodated one object, an étui or purse, and was made of silver or gold.

Buttons

Buttons come in many different materials. They were made by Wedgwood, with pale blue and white medallions, for instance, set in cut steel; by Meissen and other famous porcelain factories; and by famous French glass factories. The golden age for collectors is the 18th century; collectors may choose subjects like the French underglass habitat buttons, which have butterflies,

caterpillars and moths imprisoned in metal frames, or flowers, shells and grasses. Also under glass are the lovely paintings of 18th century ladies playing at country pursuits. Sometimes the underglass buttons sheltered paper prints of gods and goddesses. Some porcelain buttons come in sets, each with a different picture on the same subject. Men wore them rather than women in the 18th century.

Beadwork

Probably the collector will not find anything in this ancient art earlier than the 17th century, but what a satisfactory form of work it was, since those lovely colours never fade and are easily cleaned. Henry VIII wore doublets covered with beads from Venice. It is not always remembered that England was manufacturing glass beads at the beginning of the 17th century, chiefly for the purpose of selling them to the Indians in Virginia. At Jamestown Vancouver, the first glass made there was for beads for trading with the Indians.

Bead embroidery was fashionable from the 1760s' till the end of the century, when small, vivid coloured beads were on bags and waistcoats. By the 1820s even more gay colours were introduced from Venice, till by 1860 beads became large and coarse. Loomwork is recognized by the absolute uniformity of the beads, with no thread or silk showing between the horizontal rows of work. Early beads were blown and the opaque coloured ones were produced from late in the 18th century up to about 1850. Watch pockets with flowery decorations in crystal or steel or pearl, book covers, pipe-cases, tea-cosies, footstools and endless trivia for the girls to make for bazaars or Christmas presents are a feature of the 19th century beadwork. Patterns are shown in the many Domestic magazines of the period. Bugle-work, as it was called, was an American craze during the 1850s. Tubular and round glass beads were worked into freizes and patterns to decorate tablecloths, and other domestic objects.

Samplers

Among the leisure pastimes of our forebears the sampler takes the first place, being probably the earliest of these occupations. The oldest ones still in existence are at least 300 years old and were simply a kind of embroiderer's notebook. They were being made earlier still, wrote the poet, John Skelton, who was born in 1469. He refers to 'the sampler to sew on', and 'The Needle's Excellency' of the mid 17th century gives us a list of motifs used, 'Flowers, Plants, and Fishes, Beasts, Birds, Flyes and Bees'.

Samplers were stitched in France, Germany, Spain, Italy and in America. The Museum of Fine Arts in Boston has an interesting collection of needlepoint embroideries made by teenage girls dating from 1746. Their chief motif was a lady fishing and they have come to be known as the *Fishing Lady embroideries*. At the American Museum at Bath there is a charming example of a sampler, dated 1774 and worked by eleven-year-old Hannah Taylor.

Children from many countries made sampler maps, as well as free-hand pictures of their own homes, enriched by improving verses and alphabets. Darning samplers were another interesting type.

Dolls

This subject is very well documented now, especially since Georgian wooden dolls, with their primitive, stylized faces, crude limbs and enormous dark brown glass eyes, are fetching such fantastic prices both sides of the Atlantic. Wooden dolls with plaster faces and painted cheeks and eyes were made up to about 1820. Pegwoodens, papier-mâché with elaborate head-dress and later waxed papier-mâché heads, glazed china and parian heads with kid bodies, poured wax dolls, and the famous Jumeau *poupées de luxe* are all collected. The French lady doll was popular in the 1870s and then in 1880 came the *bébé* or little girl doll.

In America we think of names like Ludwig Greiner of Philadelphia, Izannah Walker who made rag dolls in the mid-19th century, Robert J Clay and his *creeping baby* of 1871 and the famous Schoenhut Company and its circus of wooden dolls. Doll-collecting in America began in earnest about 1920, according to John Noble, the Curator of the Toy Collection of the Museum of the City of New York. Musical automata are in a class by themselves, being more of an adult's toy. Acrobats and minstrels, clowns, conjurors and monkey-smokers, rabbits, birds, mechanical sea-scapes, trees and buildings with movable birds all figure in this wonderland. Collectors' pieces are rarely earlier than the beginning of the 19th century. The fabulous 18th century masterpieces are in French and English and American Museums or private collections.

Christmas cards and pictorial writing paper

In the 19th century letter-writing was still an art, and our ancestors liked to have their correspondence embellished with engravings of landscapes or stately homes, cities, or incidents in history or of topical interest. Collectors might well be advised to snap these up for they are unlikely to have a re-birth now that communications are so easy and personal letters are so few. Trade cards, which were at their best in the 18th century, are also a collectors' quarry. They served as a form of advertisement, with delicate copper engravings and elegant ornamental borders and lettering.

The various greeting cards of the 19th century were, according to Sir James Laver, first designed in 1843. He tells us that in that year Henry Cole (later the first Director of the Victoria and Albert Museum) asked John Calcott Horsley to design a card to send to his friends at Christmas.

Early Christmas cards have lacy paper borders and look rather like valentines. Marcus Ward produced splendid decorative cards designed by Walter Crane. Calendars, almanacs, New Year cards and birthday cards followed, some designed by Richard Doyle, Kate Greenaway and other well-known artists. Novelty cards were extremely elaborate with cut-out nativity scenes, and by the 1890s the comic card took the stage. Printed

ephemera covers a very wide scope and has many devotees.

Pictorial writing-paper was popular in the American Civil War, much being published by Charles Magnus of New York, who also produced Christmas cards. An early set of notepaper illustrates the signing of the Declaration of Independence. Others show famous monuments and views of cities. The issue of postcards was first authorized in Washington on 15 April 1873.

Prisoner-of-war work

Between 1756 and 1815 French, Dutch and American prisoners-of-war were confined in eleven prisons and several hulks anchored in estuaries all over England and Scotland. The prisons had markets where local tradesmen brought goods and food to sell. To earn money for these luxuries, prisoners made brilliant pieces of work from bone, straw, wood, horn and paper. French and Dutch cabinet-makers made tiny bureaux and chests with straw inlay. Ships' models, crucifixes, castles, domino boxes and mechanical toys were carved from bone, as well as chessmen and knitting sheaths, boxes, fans and so forth. Some of these various crafts were also practised by ladies of leisure of the 18th and 19th centuries, and it is hard to tell them apart.

Money boxes and miscellanea

Earthenware banks were made in most European potteries, as well as in Ohio, Pennsylvania, and New England from the 18th century onwards. There were lions and dogs, houses, birds, chests of drawers, some in the treacly brown ware of Rockingham. They were expendable, of course, but some survived.

Mechanical banks seem to have originated in America, the well-known Creedmore cast-iron ones dating from 1877; the earliest being the very heavy *hinged-man* banks of the 1840s. Britain copied them until the Americans wisely patented their designs, forcing the British craftsmen to invent their own versions. The best of them are cast-iron and they were also made in Germany and France.

Other miscellaneous antiques which may be collected include barometers, card cases, chessmen, fans, pewter, copper, tea caddies, treen, and musical instruments, to mention a few. The umbrella term *bygones* covers just about everything. Kitchen and laundry utensils, costumes and lighting all provide grist for the collectors' mill. The schoolrooms of the past had fascinating paraphernalia, too. There were hornbooks, ABCs, songs, games and scrapbooks. Portable terrestrial globes can be found, dated very early, as well as full-sized ones, and maps. Recently a collector found a mahogany box which was christened *a portable museum*. This must have been used by a travelling tutor or governess, or perhaps the village schoolmaster, to instruct pupils of the Victorian period.

Acknowledgments

180 *This table at first glance looks like Tonbridge-ware. It is in fact oriental. The mother-of-pearl inlay and the moorish-type arches at the top of the leg are the clues. It is probably Indian c. 1880.*

American Museum, Bath* **25**
Antique Dealer & Collectors' Guide **12, 67, 86, 92, 159, 161, 169, 170, 177, 178**
Asprey & Company, London **58, 61**
Ayer, London **19**
Barling, London* **11**
Baxter, HC, London* **28**
Blakemore, Kenneth **52, 53, 55, 59, 60, 63, 64, 65**
Bly, John, Tring, Herts.* **5**
Cameo Corner, London **66**
Christie, Manson & Woods, London **3, 4, 15, 23, 26, 27, 57, 94, 165**; * **6, 80, 85, 168**
Cheshire, EM, Nottingham **24**
Cooper, AC, London **39**
Corning Glass Museum, New York **155, 157, 162-164, 166, 171**
Cushion, John **116**
Delomosne, London **150**
Dennis, Richard, London **161**
Fitzwilliam Museum, Cambridge* **81, 173**
Galliner, Gabriella Gros **154**
Gentle, Rupert, Pewsey, Wilts. **176**
Godden, Geoffrey, Worthing, Sussex* **87, 91**
Goodwood House, Sussex **54**
Greenwood, WF, Harrogate, Yorks. **16**
Ham House, Surrey* **14**
King & Chasemore, Pulborough, Sussex **159**
Latham, Jean **175, 178, 179**
Mallet, London **140**; * **146**
Moss, Sidney, London* **79**
Museum of Industrial Art, Prague **151**
National Museum, Prague **152, 167**
Nordiska Museum, Stockholm **172, 174**
Parke-Bernet Galleries, New York **30, 33, 36, 38, 42, 47**
Pembroke Antiques, Hampton, Virginia **8**
Philp, Peter, Cardiff **13, 22, 83, 180**
Pinn, WA, South Dunstable, Beds.* **7**
Rolex of Geneva **50, 51**
Sack, Israel, New York **20, 21**
Sataloff, Joseph **68-78**
Sladmore Gallery, London **145**
Sotheby & Company **1, 29, 31, 32, 34, 37, 40, 41, 43, 44-46, 62, 82, 84, 90, 117-120, 124, 125-139, 141-144, 147, 165**; * **49, 89, 93, 122, 127-131**
Steppes Hill Farm Antiques **48**
Temple Newsam House, Leeds **9**
Trevor, London* **17**
Victoria & Albert Museum, London **2, 6, 35, 83, 95-112, 114, 115, 126, 148, 153, 158**; * **10, 18, 88, 123, 160**
Wartski, C & H, London **56**
William Penn Memorial Museum, Harrisburg, Penn. **113**
Wilkinson, R, London **149**

*By courtesy of the Antique Dealer & Collectors' Guide

Index